MW01687639

Mansions and Millionaires

The Remarkable Story of Maitland, Nova Scotia

John Hawkins

Nimbus Publishing

ISBN 0-88999-642-3

Copyright © 1996, 2007

All rights reserved. No part of this book may be reproduced, stored in a retrieval system or transmitted in any form or by any means without the prior written permission from the publisher, or, in the case of photocopying or other reprographic copying, permission from Access Copyright, 1 Yonge Street, Suite 1900, Toronto, Ontario M5E 1E5.

Nimbus Publishing Limited
PO Box 9166
Halifax, NS B3K 5M8
(902) 455-4286

www.nimbus.ca

Printed and bound in Canada

Cover design: Doug Porter

Previously published by Lancelot Press Limited in 1996.

Acknowledgement: This book has been published with the assistance of the Canada Council and the Nova Scotia Department of Education, Cultural Affairs Division.

Contents

To Mona

ACKNOWLEDGEMENT

I wish to thank A. Dunlop and the staff at the Nova Scotia Archives for their assistance and patience. Also Valerie Briscoe, Department of Natural Resources, as well as L.M. Richard, of the Nova Scotia Museum.

The works of Archibald MacMechan and F.W. Wallace provided much of the information relating to sea adventures and shipbuilding.

Much useful information was provided in the writings of Charles Armour of Dalhousie University.

The works and information of John Victor Duncanson were most helpful. I thank also the staff of the local museum at Selma and at Lawrence House, Maitland.

Very useful was information provided by Mr. and Mrs. Fred Roy and Mr. Roy Rhyno of Maitland.

Whatever errors or omissions which the text might contain are my own.

INTRODUCTION

The object of this book is to focus attention on a "town" that has been forgotten. Tucked away in a corner of our province on Cobequid Bay, Maitland, Hants County, was once a great shipbuilding and trading center.

Time and time again, chronicles of Nova Scotia's great shipbuilders and mastermariners revolve around citizens of Maitland and their exploits.

In current dollars, Maitland had many millionaires, and had many mansions; it had a bank, a ship's registry, and innumerable shipyards often employing a thousand men. Its captains sailed off and traded in Europe, the Orient, South America, the United States and the West Indies, and anywhere on the globe where money was to be made. Fortunes were made in selling Maitland ships, in the timber trade and in mining gypsum. In one year alone, nineteen vessels were under construction in the Maitland area.

A railway was built through South Maitland, and the Vice-President was not from New York or Ontario, but from Maitland. A six-car ferry docked at Maitland; there were tennis courts, homes furnished with the finest articles that could be purchased in the ports of the world, and Maitland also produced a number of MLA's, an executive council member and an M.P. Shipowners needed communication with the world, so a telegraph office was opened.

There was the large Commercial Hotel to accommodate visiting businessmen. In the early days there had been many taverns.

Maitland had a professional photographer to cater to the wealthy residents. It had a stagecoach and, of course, a lawyer and three Justices of the Peace. It was the "terminus" of the famous and ill-fated Shubenacadie Canal.

All these things Maitland had, yet over the years, the golden era of wooden ships and iron men lost its lustre and the economic engine that generated wealth faltered. The time of high adventure and profits gradually ended.

The halcyon days of Maitland disappeared but the heritage is not forgotten. The great homes, in the main, are as they were in the days of W.D. Lawrence. Frieze and Roy's store still operates, the buildings that housed Isaac Douglas' ironworks and Sam Murphy's livery stable are intact. Oakdale, Springhurst, and the homes of wealthy men like Alfred Putnam and W.D. Lawrence are well preserved.

Much of the past has been kept. To walk through Maitland is to take a step back in time, to the peaceful Victorian order and tranquility of the past.

The great tribune of Nova Scotia, Joseph Howe, walked these streets, campaigning for a seat in Hants County. He entered these very homes and spoke to crowds gathered in these streets. Howe House, the home of a relative, is still occupied. Here, even today, we can sense the rich heritage of our past. Maitland has been almost completely preserved; it is a town frozen in time.

Then too, there is the curious story of the Acadians, the original European settlers in the Maitland area, who built dykes and homes and raised families in relative prosperity for many generations and then, in a matter of days, disappeared from the shores of Hants forever, as a result of the Expulsion.

Their dykes and works can still be traced after hundreds of years.

Fittingly, Maitland has been recently declared a heritage conservation district by the Province of Nova Scotia and will be preserved for future generations.

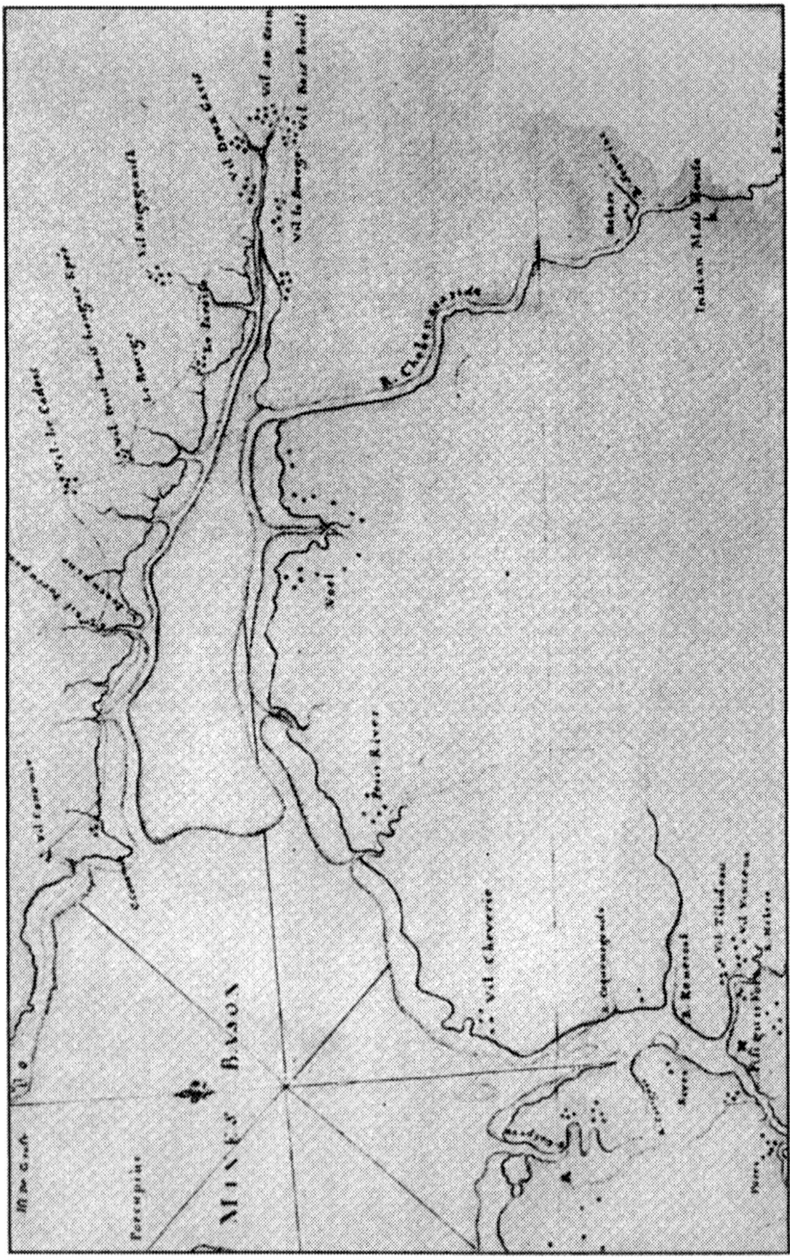

This is a map of Acadian villages (marked with dots) along the shore of the Basin and Cobequid Bay, 1756.

National Archives of Canada, H2/202-1756

CHAPTER ONE

Acadians in Hants County

FOR ALMOST thirty years it was my work to travel to the village of Hants North, to Maitland, Noel and Walton, all communities hugging the brown shores of the Cobequid Basin. In summer a cool breeze sweeps up from the tide and cools the traveller arriving over the Gore hills from the hot belly of Hants County. The brown tidal flats are in themselves a striking sight. One is impressed also by the presence of dykes, stretching along sections of shore, keeping the surging brown waters from the fertile meadows.

Here the tide reaches the highest recorded height in the world. It rushes up the Bay of Fundy, into Cobequid Basin and sweeps up the narrowing mouth of the Shubenacadie River.

The dykes, over hundreds of years, have kept out the tide, and I presumed that the stout British and American settlers had built them long ago.

A unique feature on the tidal shore is the village of Noel. The incongruity of such a name in the heart of an Anglo-Saxon county, whets the curiosity. How did the French name for Christmas exist where all is so solidly English?

Few give the matter a moment's thought, and fewer still realize that on these shores over two hundred years ago, another culture existed, totally different in habit, in language, in religion, in dwellings and all manner of life. It is recorded that 250 Acadian dwellings existed along the Hants shore. The Acadians had been settled along the Bay of Fundy since 1605.

Along the Shubenacadie River from South Maitland to Noel, a burgeoning and prosperous agricultural community existed, growing rapidly from generation to generation. Here were farms, cattle on the meadows, sheep, hogs, hundreds of children, a simple lifestyle and the Acadian culture.

Yet it all vanished without a trace, except for the few remaining dykes.

The plowmen, the housewives, the gardens, sheep in the yards, the happy laughter of Acadian life disappeared, not over a lifetime or even a decade, but within days — often in one day — never to return.

In former times the stony discipline and coldness of the English soldier struck terror into the hearts of the peace-loving Acadians. Thirty years later an English settler taking over the Acadian lands found the bones of a team of oxen secured to the yoke, the plow still buried in the furrow. Such was the haste of their departure.[1]

ACADIAN LIFE

Along the shores of the Bay of Fundy, spreading from the original settlement at Port Royal, over generations the Acadians developed virtually all the suitable marshland. Major communities were located at Windsor (Pisiquid), Grand Pré, Truro (Cobequid) and also such districts as Maitland and Noel.

What was Acadian life like in Hants County before the coming of the English? What went on along the Hants Shore before the English settlers arrived?

For well over a century, Acadians on the Bay of Fundy lived healthy and prosperous lives. At a time when only 50 percent of the general population in France reached the age of twenty-one, 75 percent reached adulthood in Port Royal.[2] And historians in general agree that the Acadian population probably doubled every twenty years between 1713 and the early 1750s.

In fact, a travelling French surgeon, Diereville, commented rather harshly in 1699: "the swarming of Brats is a sight to behold."[3] Ten or eleven children in a family were not uncommon.

The Acadian economy was based on farming, hunting and fishing, with some legal and some illegal trade taking place. In general the people lived in dwellings scattered along the shores, rather than in concentrated villages, utilizing the marshes which they dyked and cultivated.[4]

They lived in "low houses, framed of timber, and their Chimneys framed with the building of wood and lined with Clay except the fireplace. Often more than one family stayed in a single house."[5]

The Acadians who lived in the Maitland area and along the Hants shore, like all others, lived a simple life governed by the seasons, concentrating on what was grown or raised to provide food and clothing. They seemed content to live in harmony with nature. Acquisition of great wealth was not a driving force, as it was with the English settlers who followed.[6]

Acadians were great gardeners, growing an abundant variety of vegetables, including cabbage, turnips, and greens of all sorts. There is considerable debate as to whether the Acadians ever grew potatoes in Nova Scotia before 1755. They were very successful orchardists and their apple trees in Maitland and Noel Shore still existed long after English settlers arrived.

In general, their farms were small, seldom more than five to ten acres of dyked and tilled farmland within the marsh, with the orchards located in adjacent slopes.

They grew grains, such as wheat, oats, rye, barley, as well as peas, hemp and flax. Apples, pears, plums and cherries were also grown. A traveller in Acadia noted that, "finer flavored apples and greater variety, cannot in any other country be produced."[7]

Acadians were, and are, known for their thrift and economy. They raised hens, but in addition utilized the feathers for bedding. Poultry, meat and eggs were also important. Poultry was everywhere, and pigs in plenty rooted around the houses. Sheep, too, were numerous and were raised for wool, which provided clothing, as well as meat. Cows provided meat, milk and butter. A horse would be part of the farm, but oxen were also used.[8]

Down-filled mattresses were made and feathers were even exported to Louisbourg from various Acadian settlements. In fact, the Acadians of Cobequid enjoyed a standard of life often higher than some small farmers of Hants County in the twentieth century. Often there were surpluses, and the Acadians, being on the Bay could engage in export of sheep, cattle, pigs and poultry.[9] Even when under French rule, they traded with Massachusetts and New Hampshire.[10] In exchange they often received "Linnens, sail cloth, rum, molasses, wine and brandy."[11]

Their diet and life in general, therefore, was not as austere as might be imagined. Several travellers noted their liking for "fat-back" (*le lard*), which was prepared with cabbage or fried and added to vegetables."[12]

Acadian social philosophy differed sharply from that of New Englanders or later English settlers. They developed no towns, or industries. They avoided excessive regulation and government, and the basic unit was the family. Their community, however, was growing, and the growth was based on hard work and thrift.

With an abundance of fish available, Acadians also engaged in fishing with small vessels in the Bay of Fundy, and, in the case of those in Hants County, in the rivers and creeks, such as the Shubenacadie, concentrating on the harvest of salmon, shad and gaspereau.

In hunting and trapping, they learned much from their association with the Mi'kmaq. Moose was abundant and hare were caught as well as grouse. They caught beaver, fox, wolf, and marten mainly for their furs, which they frequently traded, and also used for warmth and comfort and for "beautiful cloths." They made shoes of sealskin and moosehide.[13]

It appears strange to us that the Acadians of North Hants seldom used money. It was rare for them to pay one another for services or goods. They traded labor or goods. The gold they received in trade, they stored away for future needs.[14]

An interesting story exists that seems to illustrate this point concerning the Acadians of North Hants. It is recorded in the *History of the Noel Shore:*

> There is a story that has come down from Jimmy Shad-Creek (James Densmore) which is believed to concern the Acadians. One fine summer day when William Densmore (one of the earliest British settlers of Noel Shore) was working at building his home on land near King's Creek, he and his brother saw a large sailing ship come up the bay and drop anchor off King's Creek. Some say the men were seen off the ship during the day; others said that no one got off that they saw. At any rate, no one knew what the ship was, by whom it was owned, or what was its business.
>
> One night Deacon William heard his dog barking. When the settlers went out in the morning to see the ship, she was gone. Near an old Acadian cellar by a spring on Deacon William's grant, however, they found a freshly dug excavation in the ground with a ring of rust around the inside.
>
> It was believed that the ship was some of the expelled Acadians returning to get gold which had

> been buried in a large iron pot. Nothing was ever heard of the ship again and the real explanation of the mystery will never be known.[15]

The Acadians were self-sufficient in making cloth and clothes. A French traveller, mentioned above, states that

> ... they made their own outfits, including caps and stockings. From diapers to shawls, from shirts to shifts, with considerable liking for mixing black with red for ornament, and binding their skirts with ribbons, the Acadians spun, wove, knitted and sewed their garments.[16]

While most families were self-sufficient, grains were usually ground at grist mills, as was the case in Cheticamp, Cape Breton, as late as the 1930s. Bread was the staple of Acadian diet.

Children were well cared for and records exist of a child's rattle being made from a dried pig's bladder filled with peas and hung so an infant could bat it about and watch it swing.[17]

Like today's Acadians they enjoyed merrymaking. A priest's report of the Archdiocese of Quebec of 1742 inferred that there was drinking on Sundays. The report condemned some Acadian communities that allowed men and women not only to dance together after sunset but even permitted singing of "lascivious songs."

The Acadians were religious but by no means fanatical or austere in their conduct. Because of the scattered settlements, religious activities were less formal than in the twentieth century. There were, for instance, no stone churches built by Acadians before 1755.

The Acadians were skilled craftsmen, particularly in woodcarving. They made tools, furniture and utensils from the wood of the local forest. Yet despite their obvious industry and many talents, in the years immediately before the expulsion, few seemed to have had any formal education. Many signed by marking an X. Apart from the education provided in the beginning by priests, little effort seems to have been spent on academic learning. In contrast, English settlements usually established schools very early.

In Acadia, education was conducted independently by the family itself and the subject matter involved practical skills in heading up a home and family and providing for children. Few children were able to receive any schooling.[18]

The Acadians were remarkably healthy. They lived in a clean and uncluttered environment and had a good and varied supply of nutritious food. In addition, there is evidence to indicate they knew the medicinal value of certain plants. This information they were given by the Mi'kmaq.

As early as 1671, a French missionary, Father Laurent Molins, conducted a census, and enumerated several individuals over sixty and "one man, Jehan Gaudet, who was 93."[19]

Between 1713 and 1755, the Acadians enjoyed good health, prosperity, and a burgeoning population. But the Golden Age of Acadian life was soon to come to an abrupt end.

THE EXPULSION

Such was the happy pattern of Acadian life that existed for over a hundred years, before a series of events altered their tranquil and productive existence, and removed forever their culture and their progeny from the shores of Hants County.

Several factors conspired to bring about the extinction of Acadian life in Hants during the middle years of the 1700s. During this period a state of war frequently existed between Great Britain and France. War and battles in other quarters of the world focused attention on the French living in Nova

Scotia. Britain, and British colonists in New England, feared the presence of French Acadians in such close proximity.

In addition, the powerful Fortress of Louisbourg was in French hands, and Acadians frequently supplied the French with food and other supplies.

It must be remembered, too, that in 1750 Acadians on mainland Nova Scotia numbered ten thousand, far outnumbering British settlers. While it is easy now to evaluate their political philosophy, their loyalty in time of war presented a real fear for British officials.

Ross and Deveau in *The Acadians of Nova Scotia* point out that the British on several occasions had conflicts with Mi'kmaq, and Acadians were viewed as being closely associated with the natives.

These factors probably meant little to the Acadians living at Noel and Maitland. Distant wars to them were as remote as the moon is to us today. Their concerns were their own farms and families, not affairs in London or Paris. They were not political, and I believe were essentially neutral, wishing to avoid conflict with English, French and Mi'kmaq. That, however, was not to be.

"On July 28, 1755, the Chief Justice of Nova Scotia, Jonathan Belcher, addressed Governor Lawrence and the Council at Halifax. At the end of a long submission on the conduct of the Acadians, Chief Justice Belcher stated that he was 'obliged ... to advise that all the French inhabitants may be removed from the Province.' "[20]

One source of mischief was Louis Joseph LeLoutre, vicar general of Acadian and missionary to the Mi'kmaq. He was a part-time resident of his headquarters at the native settlement at Shubenacadie. His mission headquarters, many felt, was the source of much plotting against the English. It is also said he was a malevolent influence upon the Mi'kmaq and intimidated the Acadians and their clergy.

However, LeLoutre probably felt he was just doing his

job. He was clever, energetic, and tireless.

This strange priest, living among the Indians on the banks of the Shubenacadie River a few miles from Maitland, was the first clergyman to preach the word of God to citizens of East Hants.

Reverend T. Chalmers Jack, in 1903, stated at Maitland: "Toward the Acadians he was a despot; and this simple and superstitious people ... trembled before him."[21] LeLoutre played a substantial part in fuelling the ill feeling that existed between the English government and the Acadians.

On August 11, 1755, at Fort Beausejour, the deportation began. Acadians were rounded up and imprisoned in the Fort before being shipped to the eastern British colonies, now the United States.

One month later Col. John Winslow moved on Grand Pré and ordered the male inhabitants into the church of Saint Charles des Mines at three o'clock on September 5.

At Pisiquid (Windsor) similar operations were carried out by Captain Alexander Murray who told Acadians that their lands, houses, and livestock would be confiscated and that they and their families would be transported out of the province.[22] Their homes, in most cases, were burned to prevent any chance of resettlement.

SOME ACADIANS ESCAPE

The terror and grief of these scenes are unique in the history of Hants County. Homes occupied for generations, orchards, gardens, fields and dykes, gained by generations of labor; cattle, sheep and all livestock and possessions were lost. Husbands, wives and children were often separated and scattered. The desolation of that day, in what are now the quiet villages of Hants County, can only be imagined.

An Acadian, Mr. Nicolas Gautier of Port Royal, was engaged in trade and owned seven small ships, which travelled to the various Acadian settlements including those of Noel and surrounding areas as well as Isle St. Jean (PEI). When Gautier arrived back at Port Royal in August, 1755, he found its homes in flames and the British in possession of the the settlement.

Gautier kept his cannon trained on the British garrison, and, abandoning his sails because of the difficulty of hoisting them, he had his crew man the oars and back the vessel out into Digby Gut. By this strategy he escaped, and realizing that all Acadian settlements were in danger, he headed up the Bay of Fundy to warn them.

It is recorded that this intrepid sailor landed at Salter's Head, (Selma, Hants County) and informed a friend and business associate, Mr. Amand Bugeau of the danger.[23] Bugeau was a "wealthy" and influential Acadian who lived there.[24]

Bugeau informed the inhabitants that British forces would arrive there within two weeks to take them prisoner and destroy their homes. He told the people to abandon their homes and meet him in Tatamagouche, for he had already made arrangements with Gautier to have his ships prepared at that port to take the local Acadians to PEI (Isle St. Jean) where they might resettle in safety, and where other Acadians were already established.

Hearing the fearful stories of imprisonment and deportation at Port Royal, the Acadians of the Noel settlement and Ville Robert, (known today as Maitland district) departed in great haste.

They left their homes and many possessions, often cattle and livestock — even oxen still in the yoke. In at least one case a modest store of gold was left buried on the farmsite.

Some left by boat, others took the exhausting overland trail across the backbone of Nova Scotia to Tatamagouche.[25] It must have been a pitiful sight; mothers, children and the aged packed their movable belongings and left the land they had worked and the homes they had lived in for generations.

All local Acadians were not so fortunate as those who departed early. Some did not heed the warning or could not bring themselves to leave.

September 4 was the fateful day for the Acadians of what is now known as North Hants. On that day the hearts of those who remained must have sunk as they looked across the Bay and saw Acadian homes on fire in the settlement at Cobequid and Masstown. Most then left and it appears that most escaped.

Two days before on Tuesday, September 2, 1775, on the afternoon tide, three British vessels had been seen sailing up the Bay. The fear mounted for Acadians as one ship anchored within sight, opposite Masstown.

On the door of Cobequid Catholic church, a substantial building of one hundred feet by forty, which could be clearly seen from Selma, Captain John Winslow posted his famous notice, which applied to Acadians of both sides of the Bay.

Reverend T. Chalmers Jack, B.A., in a talk at Maitland in 1903 quoted the notice:

> "To the inhabitants of the village of Cobequid, and the surrounding shores, as well ancient as young men and lads." He ordered them all to repair to the church next day, Wednesday, September 3 at three p.m. to hear what he had to say to them. From this side the ringing of the large bell of Father Gerard's Church would easily be heard, and perhaps also the accompaning drum beat of the English Soldiery that day.[26]

Rev. Jack continues:

> Before September's first Sunday, that sad year, desolation reigned in every French settlement and home on these shores. Those of our immediate surroundings were put on ship-board at Selma, those of Noel from their own shores.[27]

Reverend Jack pointed out that 250 buildings were destroyed along the Shubenacadie River and Bay.

Yet all was not destroyed. LeLoutre's Mass House at Shubenacadie survived. Reverend Jack tells us that "Indians and French rallied to save it, attacking the English and killing or wounding some thirty of them, drove the rest to their boats."[28]

Some at Salter's Head, Selma, were not so fortunate as others. Because of a stand of trees they did not see the homes of Masstown burning and were not informed. The British landed and captured all who had not fled.

The local Acadian leader, Amand Bugeau, financed the settlement of "Noel shore" area Acadians in Tracadie, PEI. Nicolas Gautier supplied transportation as agreed, under the direction of Bugeau who also purchased supplies for those leaving. Bugeau was well informed on such matters since he had travelled widely between Acadia and Isle St. Jean. About one hundred families were moved to Isle St. Jean between 1743 and 1758.

A local Acadian, Noel Pinet from Noel, settled at Pinette, PEI, in 1738 and was followed by Gaudets and Brodettes two or three years later.[29]

In the French census of 1707, for the district of Cobequid familiar Acadian names occur. The writing on the old documents is not always clear, but several keep recurring. Some are as follows: Martin Blachard, Martin Bourg (Bourk), Jean Hebert, and Marie Landry, Gerauls Guirin and Isabelle Aucoin, Germain Cherroir and Marie Morin, Joseph Douaft and Clair Bourg.

Some of these people, no doubt, lived in the Maitland-Noel area or settled there after 1707. There were at the time of the Acadian expulsion about ten thousand French living in mainland Nova Scotia. It must be remembered, however, that Acadians were very tenacious people with a strong attachment to the land. Ross and Deveau tell us that there were six thousand Acadians deported to the Anglo-American colonies of Massachusetts, Connecticut, New York, Pennsylvania, Maryland, Virginia, and Carolina. Amazingly, by the beginning of the 1800s, more than 70 percent of Acadians had resettled in the Maritimes and Quebec.[30]

None, however, returned to the mighty tides, high cliffs and brown clay flats of Hants shore, save one. In 1988, I met a man living alone in the area of Maitland-Selma, by the name of Bellfountaine. Without doubt, he was an Acadian, but I suspect from the Chezzetcook area, who had none-the-less, perhaps by chance, re-established an Acadian presence in the former home of his ancestors.

"The large bell of LeLoutre's church at Shubenacadie," one which could be heard betimes, legend says, the whole length of the river, "was put into the lake (Snide's) for safe keeping." No record of the bell being recovered exists.[31]

Reverend Jack reports in 1903 on the remaining works of the Acadians:

> Fruit trees were recently, if they are not yet to be seen here and there, where the French planted them. The lines of their dykes are still to be seen ... Only a few years since in the marsh nearby, the late W.D. Lawrence used to show one of their sluiceways, the wood of the pine tree still solid some one hundred and thirty years after the race of these who felled and hauled and hewed it had been sent from the possession of the lands they so wisely selected... French field, a pretty nook, is still called, not over a mile away, at the head of the Selma Marsh. The yet unfilled hollows that tell of the cellars once covered by their houses are still pointed out "manywhere" along the shores of the Shubenacadie and the waters of the Minas into which it flows.[32]

Between that fateful day in September 1755 and 1763,

the rich marshlands, the orchards, wells and dykes, for all practical purposes, were forgotten — except perhaps for a passing Mi'kmaq who might have noticed with contempt the ephemeral nature of the works of Europeans.

The cattle in the meadows had vanished; the laughter of the frolicking children was silent; the bustling madam of the habitation had disappeared. The warm sun of August beat down, the cool breeze swept up from the Bay. Salmon, shad, gaspereau swam on their annual journey up the Bay and into the Shubenacadie River. But the settlements on the shores, the homes of the Acadians, were gone and would never return.

Man and his works, however, like other forms of life, are not easily extinguished — especially when there are opportunities and rewards, such as are provided by productive lands, forests and a fishery.

The years rolled by and other men sensed an opportunity in the land which they would name Hants County, and upon which they would place the stamp of their culture. That would come in 1763, less than ten years after the departure of the Acadians. Out of the ashes, another society and culture would arise. It was a new beginning. A bright future lay ahead.

NOTES

1. *History of Noel Shore*, Noel Shore Women's Institute, 1959, p. 12.
2. Naomi Griffiths, "The Golden Age: Acadian Life, 1713-1748," *Social History*, Vol. XVII, No. 33, May, 1984, p. 23.
3. *Ibid.*, p. 26
4. *Ibid.*, p. 27.
5. *Ibid.*
6. *Ibid.*
7. *Ibid.*, pp. 27, 31.
8. *Ibid.*
9. *Ibid.*, p. 28.
10. *Ibid.*
11. *Ibid.*
12. *Ibid.*
13. *Ibid.*
14. *Ibid.*
15. *History of Noel Shore*, p. 13.
16. Griffiths, p. 30.
17. *Ibid.*, p. 31.
18. Ross, Sally; Alphonse Deveau; *The Acadians of Nova Scotia*, Nimbus, 1992, p. 49.
19. *Ibid.*, p 30.
20. *The Acadians of Nova Scotia*, p. 61.
21. Maitland Centennial Celebration (1803-1903), June 21, 1903, p. 48.
22. *The Acadians of Nova Scotia*, p. 61.
23. *History of Noel Shore*, p. 12.
24. *Ibid.*

25. *Ibid.*

26. Maitland Centennial Celebration, p. 49.

27. *Ibid.*

28. *Ibid.*

29. *History of Noel Shore*, p. 12.

30. *The Acadians of Nova Scotia*, pp. 63, 65.

31. Maitland Centennial Celebrations, p. 49.

32. *Ibid.*, p. 47.

CHAPTER TWO

MAITLAND, THE BEGINNING

We have followed the history of Maitland from the first settlers, perhaps not as important as some larger places, but never-the-less, dear to the hearts of those who have spent their lives there.

— Abbie Lawrence, *History of Maitland*

ALTHOUGH THE early residents of Maitland and area frequently inherited lands that had been cultivated by the Acadians, the early years were by no means easy. It is evident that the outlook and ambitions of the two cultures were entirely different. Acadian life was centered around the land, the family and peaceful life. New England and British settlers, while valuing religion and family, were a questing race, always seeking to progress and build, and looking outward to the Empire and the world.

In addition to establishing churches, these settlers cultivated learning and established schools. Not satisfied with subsistence farming, they engaged in resource industries like cutting timber, mining gypsum, and shipbuilding. They were driven by the Anglo-Saxon ambition of the time. Were they happier than the Acadians? I doubt it. But with a keen sense of achievement and optimism, in the next century they would acquire more wealth, initiate more industry, construct greater mansions, dream greater dreams, than their Acadian predecessors.

They started modestly and in small numbers. Their success in establishing a settlement was at first by no means certain, since they did not have the local skills or knowledge of the Acadians. Nor did they always have the support of the Mi'kmaq which the Acadians had enjoyed.

FIRST GRANTS

The first grants of land in the area, of course, followed the pattern of Acadian development along the Shubenacadie River. The first English grants along the river were on the Colchester side in 1763, eight years after the departure of the French.

Henry and Francis Ellis received a grant in 1765. The Salter brothers, Malachy and Montague, whose name is still commemorated on the point of land at Salter's head, Selma, received a grant on the Hants County side in 1766. Hon. Malachy Salter was a prominent Nova Scotian, and Salter Street in Halifax bears his name. Salter had a grant of 2,000 acres with a sea frontage of four miles at Selma. He never lived upon the land.[1]

Early settlers up-river bore the names Frame, Moore, Nelson, Woodworth, Dart and Pollock, some from New England and Ireland, by way of Windsor and Horton.

The country between Maitland and Shubenacadie was taken up by Scotsmen, Highlanders and Lowlanders, often veterans of the Navy and Army. The first settler in Urbania was Donald Rose, an Inverness-shire man. George Main, a lowland Scottish soldier, established himself at South Maitland, where the first church was later built.[2]

The Camerons, still known in Hants, came from Pictou County and had their first Hants ancestors in Alex and William. William married the daughter of Allan MacArthur, a

British soldier who had fought at Bunker Hill.

The first English settler in the Maitland area was John Ranes, a Cornhill, Massachusets man. The name survives in Cape Cod and elsewhere. He was the ancestor of all who bear the name Rhines,[3] and "his first house stood on a knoll just this side of the foundry site" and built on an old Acadian cellar.

PUTNAM COMES TO MAITLAND

The first grant in Maitland was that of William Putnam and his stepfather, Luke Upham, dated Jaunary 30, 1771. Elizabeth Frame writes that he had a grant of a few hundred acres, and "upon this lot stands the present "town" of Maitland. William and Caleb Putnam chopped "a field and built the first house in the town."[4] William Frieze, who built a store, came from Providence, Rhode Island.

Not far away, at Noel, the family of Timothy O'Brien was the first to settle. They left Londonderry, Ireland in 1769 and descendants reside in that village today. His land was inherited by four sons: Robert, Isaac, Andrew and Jacob.

The Densmore family, also of Londonderry, arrived about the same time — James, Francis, Samuel and William. From the North of Ireland area were the Faulkners and McLellans. They settled along the Hants Shore area. An early Hants settler also was Andrew Main, "a Ship Hector, Scotchman, from Dunfermline."[5]

LIEUTENANT COLONEL JOHN SMALL

Though only peripherally associated with Maitland, the heroic figure of Colonel John Small and the 84th Regiment of Foot (Royal Highland Emigrant Regiment) commands mention, since their role in the history of East Hants is most important.

General John Small (1726-1796) commander of 2nd Battalion, Royal Highland Emigrants (84th Regiment).
Watercolour, National Archives of Canada, No. c-2164.

Colonel Small bought the property granted to Malachy Salter and erected a grand house on a forest-covered hill overlooking the Cobequid Bay. In the days of log houses, his home, called Selma Hall, had fittings and furniture brought from England. There the Colonel lived for six years.

In 1790, however, he returned to England, leaving a tenant, one "McCollom," in charge of Selma. Soon after his departure his fine home, Selma Hall, became the prey of flames and the Colonel never returned.[6]

The recruits for the 2nd Battalion of the Regiment were from a variety of locations: North Carolina, Boston, Prince Edward Island, Newfoundland and Scotland.

As to the final years of Colonel Small (1726-1796), his conspicuous bravery and ability were not forgotten. Shortly before his return to England, he was appointed Adjutant

General of the Nova Scotia Militia with the provincial rank of brigadier. After living in retirement in Britain he was appointed Lieutenant-Governor of the Isle of Guernsey. His promotion to major-general was dated October 3, 1794. He died at Guernsey on March 17, 1796.

HANTS TO BE FEUDAL BARONIES

Colonel Small's Hants County lands at Selma and Amherstford (Kennetcook) were inherited by his cousin, General John Reid. Small's will is on file in London, England, and reflects his keen interest in his Scottish heritage. He made provisions in the will for the establishment of two feudal baronies in Hants County, Nova Scotia. One was to be the Barony of Stralock to preserve the ancient title of General Reid's family and the other was to be the Barony of Dinenean... "to perpetuate the name of Small, originally descended from the ancient and gallant race of Douglas."

Of course, Small's plans for feudal land holdings in Hants County did not materialize. His executors sold the lands on the Kennetcook and Shubenacadie Rivers and the monies from the sale were added to General Reid's funds which amounted to £73,000, when bequeathed to the University of Edinburgh.[7]

Rev. Jack writes of the great man who led the ancestors of many residents now living in East Hants:

> No chief of former days ever more firmly secured the attachment of his clans, and no chief certainly ever deserved it better. With enthusiasm and almost romantic love of his country and his countrymen, it seemed as if the principal object of his life had been to serve them and promote their prosperity. Equally brave in leading them to the field, and kind and just and conciliating in quarters, they would have indeed, been

ungrateful if they had regarded him otherwise than they did. There was not an instance of desertion in the battalion.

Colonel Small had commanded the 2nd Battalion of the 84th Regiment which had fought at Bunker Hill and through "actual war" for seven years.[8]

The gallantry of the men of the 84th in the Revolutionary War in the U.S. was not forgotten. Colonel Small saw to it that "promises of two hundred acres of land for each soldier and fifty for each of his family besides" were fulfilled by the Nova Scotia government. Thus the basis of landholding of these veterans in East Hants was assured.

While Colonel Small settled in the Maitland area, the bulk of his men settled in the Gore, Nine Mile River and Kennetcook area.[9]

Key men in his command were Captain McLean who lived at McLean's Brook, Lieutenant Robert Robertson, and Mungo Campbell whose home was at what is now known as Mungo's Brook.[10]

Some non-commissioned officers of that day were: Sergeant Major Alexander Fraser, Sergeants McDougall and McKay, and Drum Major Job Ross. Serving soldiers included names such as Grant, Furgeson, McDonald, Miller, Cameron, McArthur, Rafter, Gill and McPhee. Many of these names still survive in East Hants today.

They were allowed two years' rations. Captain McLean, who was in charge of the commissariat, kept a diary and set up his residence on the Kennetcook River. It was named Mundungus Hall.[11]

Elizabeth Frame notes that the first Protestant clergyman (presumably in Kennetcook and Nine Mile River) was Reverend Edmund Chapman Willoughby. Subscribing supporters at that early date had surnames still common in East Hants today: Eleanor Maclean, William Smith, James

Campbell, Lewis Ettinger, Donald McDougall, Alex McDonald, Alex McPhee, Thomas Laften (probably Laffin today), Daniel Thompson, Alex Furgeson, Duncan McArthur, Christian Henegar, Abraham Blois, James Fraser, Donald Grant, William Singer, among others. Those who still bear those surnames may have roots that go back to the very beginnings of Hants County. Indeed, to before there was a Hants County.

NOTES

1. Rev. Jack, Maitland Centennial Celebrations, 1903, p. 50 (PANS).
2. *Ibid.*
3. *Ibid.*
4. Frame, Elizabeth, "History of East Hants," mss., p. 3, PANS.
5. *Ibid.*
6. *Ibid.*, p. 5.
7. Duncanson, John, *The Loyalist Township of Nova Scotia*, Mica Publishing Co., Belleville, Ont., 1989, pp. 63-72.
8. Frame, *Ibid.*
9. *Ibid.*, p. 4
10. Jack, p. 52
11. Duncanson, p. 68.

CHAPTER THREE

EARLY MAITLAND

IN 1903, during the centennial celebrations of the induction of Reverend Alexander Dick on June 21, 1803, it was noted that "Mouth of the River" was the original name of Maitland. The name Maitland was given in honour of Sir Peregrine Maitland, who was Governor of Nova Scotia from 1828 to 1834.

Abbie Lawrence tells us that in 1813, there were eleven houses in the village "and four of them were taverns."[1] I suspect the term taverns refers more to lodging houses rather than drinking dens, though liquor might have been served.

In 1831 there was one store — that of James Whidden. The Whiddens originally came from Truro and were engaged in shipbuilding.[2] A Whidden House (c. 1850) still exists in Maitland.

Miss Lawrence also mentions the store of a Mr. Cochrane who presumably came later. The building, which housed a Cochrane's store, still exists in the village.

In 1832, the mail was delivered once a month by a Mr. Nathan Smith, who was the first carrier and came on horseback via Newport and the Kennetcook valley and carried the mail in his pocket.[3] The first post office was built in 1846 and was operated by Mr. Adam Roy.

As mentioned, in 1803 the first ordained minister,

Cochrane's store, built circa 1860, as it looks today. Honourable Arthur Cochrane, MLA, was a local merchant and shipbuilder. In politics he was a member of the Legislative Council of Nova Scotia, and in the Provincial Cabinet from 1882 to 1883.

Reverend Alexander Dick, came to Maitland and his congregation was known as Douglas.

The first school was on the site of the Putnam Brother's Store. The seats were of planks, with sticks for legs. In the beginning the teachers, Miss Lawrence tells us, were not very good, usually disbanded soldiers. One good teacher was Adam Roy.[4]

Elizabeth Frame records that "houses of round logs, notched at the corners, the floors of hewn stuff," were standard. The new settlers were not much advanced from the Acadians they replaced. "In such houses, the inmates burned their faces by the fire to keep from freezing, and sometimes watched by turns to keep the huge fires from dying out."[5]

In time these were replaced by shingled dwellings. They had latches and hinges of wood and chimneys built of small round wood, well plastered, or "hatted" with clay. Frame gives a stark picture of the home life of the Hants pioneer wife and her furnishings.

> Sometimes a chimney would not draw, and a board had to be hung below the mantel piece to keep in the smoke. This prevented the sight of the stars, through the wide chimney top.
>
> The unsavory dye tub ... stood in the corner; the light from the ample fire shone on the dresser with its plates standing on their edges; the (spinning) wheel and cards seldom idle, were plied, by its cheerful light. Reading or work often went on without the aid of a tallow dipped candle.
>
> Brooms were made of birch twigs or splits, the floors were well sanded, and then the sand swept in various figures. A bed was usually seen in one corner of the room often high-posted, with a home made curtain, and in the day time, a trundle bed was shoved beneath it.
>
> For livestock, log hovels gave place to barns, often colder than the hovel. Here the flax was dressed, as the process of breaking, scutching, and hatcheling was called. It was made into twine for nets.
>
> Every house had not a loom, yet cloth for bedding, table and family was woven out of the linen and woolen yarn.
>
> The maple tree supplied fuel, sugar and soap to these industrious pioneers.[6]

Frame makes a concluding comment:

> How well their descendents have succeeded since 1810 may be seen in the well tilled fields, their fine dwellings, their ships, commodious school houses, and in all the evidences of an intelligent and prosperous people.[7]

It would certainly appear then, that the struggles of the early Maitland pioneers were little different from those of the Acadians. In fact their lives may have been more difficult, since they were not always accustomed to such hardships.

When we evaluate the enormous sacrifices of the military families who finally settled here, when we reflect on the grinding struggles of these pioneers to wrest a life from the land, we should be proud of the heritage they left us.

WOMEN'S ROLE

Particularly significant is the commanding role played by pioneer women. When we consider the lives of pioneer homemakers in Hants County our reaction must be one of respect and awe. Often coming from cities, or at least semi-civilized areas of Britain and America, they were cast into the wilderness, often in isolation, as very young girls.

Theirs were tiny log homes, drafty and cold in winter, hot and mosquito-ridden in summer. Making a home in these circumstances was their role. Prolific childbearing, often with ten or more children, without the assistance of doctors, nurses or hospitals was often the norm.

Cooking before a fireplace, handling logs and chimney pots, tending fires, sewing, knitting, weaving, trying to keep such smoky cabins clean, and above all providing nurturing comfort for the ever-growing family of children in a one-room cabin, as well as providing a home for the husband who was struggling to put bread on the table — that was their life.

Are there any words adequate to praise these pioneer mothers of our province, these builders of our culture and heritage? Hopefully, their achievements will never be forgotten.

In 1830, the pioneers lived hard lives, but the golden age was soon to come — the time when the iron men of this area would build their massive wooden ships and sail them to the four corners of the world. Instead of poverty and the struggle to survive, there would be wealth and prosperity.

NOTES

1. Lawrence, Abbie, *History of Maitland*, P.A.N.S.
2. McKiel, Rex, East Hants Historical Society, March 13, 1973.
3. Lawrence, *Ibid.*
4. *Ibid.*
5. Frame. p. 16.
6. *Ibid.*
7. *Ibid.*

CHAPTER FOUR

FROM PIONEER SETTLEMENT TO TOWN

NAPOLEON BONAPARTE, the great general and emperor of France, was a dominant world figure in the early nineteenth century. His mesmeric powers as a leader could galvanize a demoralized rabble into an inspired fighting force and lift a dispirited nation from depression to the brink of world domination.

Yet how could such a man, thousands of miles from Maitland, Hants County, where English settlers struggled merely to keep food in their modest cabins, alter and transform their primitive existence?

Nothing creates work like war. Fortunes are made and lost as the tides of war shift between adversaries, and resources, materials, men are required to fuel the engines of military hostilities.

War as we have seen affected the former residents of North Hants, the Acadians, to their detriment. Now, the titanic struggle between French and British empires, between "Boney," the French dictator, and his British military adversaries, Horatio Nelson and Churchill's great ancestor, the Duke of Wellington, were being played out on the world stage. This would benefit the little settlement in Hants known as the "Mouth of the River," later known as Maitland.

War would affect the settlers in ways they could never imagine, as they toiled clearing their fields and raising their children. A town was to be created. The little hamlet would give rise to a sophisticated society of world travellers, traders, wealthy men with mansions and servants, bankers, shipbuilders and politicians, who would flourish in a golden age of sail, prosper for a time and then vanish, leaving the passing tourist to gaze in wonder at the magnificent homes that line the streets of the once prosperous "town" of Maitland.

How did this wealth come about? How did it all disappear?

BEGINNINGS OF INDUSTRY

Talent and hard work, no doubt, play an important role in the generation of wealth, but good fortune, or plain luck, is also a vital ingredient. The seed must fall in fertile soil to grow and prosper.

World events in the nineteenth century transpired to generate a growing demand for timber. The building of warships, housing for naval facilities, expansion in the United States, and the exhaustion of timber supplies in other quarters of the world, made timber a very valuable resource.

Let us turn to an authority on such matters. Charles Armour and Thomas Lackey, in their book *Sailing Ships*, give some insight into why the timber trade grew in Nova Scotia and in Hants County: "During the Napoleonic Wars, the duty on timber imported to Britain from Europe had been very high, while colonial timber was imported almost duty-free."[1] The result was a rapid increase in the importation of timber from the colonies. In addition the postwar period saw substantial increases in timber prices. It created a demand for Nova Scotia timber and for vessels to carry timber.

That impenetrable green wall of virgin timber — spruce, pine, fir, birch, maple, beech and oak — which the Acadians avoided, and the British settlers strove to clear for fields, suddenly became a valuable asset. There were thousands of acres of it.

AMERICAN AGRICULTURE

After the American Revolution in 1776, wheat and flour remained the principal exports from the Middle and Southern states of the United States. Unfortunately the land there had lost much of its original fertility, and without a constant addition of fertilizer it would not yield an average crop.[2]

In the latter years of the 1700s gypsum, an important ingredient of fertilizer, became essential to the thriving agricultural industry. If it could be landed at the Eastern U.S. seaports, there was a profitable market. By good fortune, and unlike some other areas of Hants, the Maitland settlers in fact lived at a seaport, with the highest tides in the world which would float great seagoing vessels.

A GYPSUM FIND

Settlers were often discouraged with their grants of land which were marred by strange hills made of a curious, soft white rock from South Maitland to Maitland. The land was impossible even to walk over, to plow, or to pasture cattle on, and dangerous also because of deep sinkholes. Ironically, in the early 1800s, the junk pasture became very valuable, and the rough hills, it was found, were composed of a substance desperately wanted by many farmers, particularly Americans — gypsum. To some penniless settlers, living from their scant crops, it was a bonanza. Gypsum was white gold. Known as plaster rock or land plaster, it was worth a fortune to the farmers of the Eastern United States.

WHITE GOLD — GYPSUM

The discovery of gypsum, and the realization of its economic viability as an industry for the settlers of North Hants, must have been as exciting as the discovery of gold at Renfrew over sixty years later. To cash-hungry pioneers, it was as good as gold.

In the publication *Agricultural History*, author Gerald Graham records:

> gypsum, ... proved to be an unexcelled calcium fertilizer for use in the production of grain in the days before more efficient chemical compounds were available.[3] Hence, beginning with the later years of the eighteenth century, gypsum became an essential article of import to the States. Quarried with the aid of gunpowder, the hard dirty-grayish masses of gypsum, were broken up and carried in small boats down the rivers and inlets to the American border at Passamaquoddy Bay. There New England vessels loaded the cargoes, which were ultimately received free of duty in such ports as Boston.

Whether Hants gypsum took that exact route, is not clear, but obviously a burgeoning market developed, which greatly influenced many Hants gypsum producing areas, such as Maitland.

GYPSUM RISES — $4.00 TO $36.00

Sometimes good fortune bestows its riches unexpectedly. Thus it was in many Hants County communities in those early years. Gerald S. Graham outlines the developments: "It (gypsum), is necessary to agriculture in the United States to so great a degree," wrote the British consul at Baltimore, "as to make the value of their lands entirely dependent upon it. Without it," he added, "the value of the lands in Maryland would sink, 50 percent."

But not even the American businessmen involved could have anticipated the turn of events that would create an even greater cash return.

Graham writes: "Worth on an average of about $4.00 a ton when first shipped, a price which yielded a liberal profit to the small proprietors who handled it, gypsum was known to rise, on one occasion at least, to as much as $36.00 a ton in the United States, improving most decidedly," in the words of the British traveller, "the diminished fertility of the soil of the United States."[4]

Few things create more excitement than money. Gold perhaps is one, romance another. But as Ecclesiastes tells us, "Wine maketh merry, but money answereth all things." The prospect of wealth, where there had been none before, wealth lying in pasture and forests, had a decidedly exciting and energizing effect.

And the gypsum market was booming. At the beginning of the nineteenth century, the annual import of gypsum to the United States was 30,000 tons. It soon climbed to 100,000 tons, and in terms of pounds sterling, it amounted to more than all the rest of the British North American imports combined ... and the chief exporting towns of the Maritimes lay at the head of the Bay of Fundy, close to the gypsum quarries.[5]

Graham writes: "From little villages ... small craft, manned chiefly by countrymen who neglected their farms for the more profitable industry, made one or two trips each year to the boundary, returning home laden with teas, coarse cottons, spirits, shoes and boots, and other ... goods."

Usually under thirty tons burden, such vessels could coast along the shores in shallow water.[6] Few if any, records exist relating to the voyages of these small vessels out of the Bay of

Fundy, and indeed many may not have wished to be recorded by customs officials. But it may be presumed by the above records, that Hants North and such ports as Maitland and Noel, benefited substantially from the production of gypsum.

MAITLAND, ELEVEN HOUSES

Abbie Lawrence tells us that in 1813 there were eleven houses in Maitland. She also records that during those early years "people were principally engaged in shipping plaster to the U.S. and building coastal vessels to carry it."[7]

From these early beginnings, Maitland became something of a trading center, with boatmen coming downriver from Stewiacke to do trading in Maitland during the period around 1831.

Often, hardwood and squared timber also would be sold.[8] Whidden's "large" store was established about this time and we may presume that through trading in commodities such as gypsum and timber, various necessities would be brought in both from St. John and further points, such as the United States.

Miss Lawrence concludes that "most started with smaller vessels and then as opportunities grew, built larger ships, and so prosperity and increased work was achieved."[9]

JOHN GRAHAM STARTS A QUARRY

When the East Hants Historical Society met at Maitland, November 14, 1972, Mr. Rex McKiel, a local historian, stated that the French had a settlement at South Maitland and remains of their dykes could still be seen there. Their farms were resettled by MacDougalls, Grahams and MacQueens.

"John Graham was known as 'The Governor.' In 1813 he built a large home known as 'the Mansion' ..." Mr. MacKiel is specific on an important point. "John Graham, the elder,

John Graham (March 1775-1862) and his daughter Clarissa Adelia (Mrs. Nelson Murphy) 1833-1889.

opened the White Rock Quarry and thousands of tons were quarried there." We may be permitted to speculate that at least part of Mr. Graham's fortune was based on the trade of gypsum.

Journalist Hattie Densmore, records that Graham, from the "Highlands of Scotland," in the latter part of the 1700s, was one of the first men to "develop the gypsum industry in Hants County. He opened the one-time famous White Rock Quarry and his industry flourished until the Civil War in the United States."[10]

John Graham became a very wealthy man. He was born in 1775 and died in 1862. His home, referred to as "the Mansion" was one of the largest in Hants County. Built all of pine, it had immense timbers, the sills being fourteen inches square. The house had five fireplaces and it is said each would "take a cart load of wood." The basement of this home was once used as a school.

"The Governor," as he was known, shipped hundreds of thousands of tons of gypsum from White Rock Quarry and was one of the first to engage in shipbuilding.

His daughter, Clarissa, married Nelson Murphy, who was the first Warden of East Hants.

The gypsum industry, although overshadowed today by stories of shipbuilding, was not a mere flash in the pan. It provided employment for at least half a century, and indeed is still a thriving industry in Windsor and Milford, Hants County. Today's operations, however, because of economies of scale and mechanization, dwarf the old quarries in production. Still, in their day, the quarries of South Maitland, Noel and Walton were pivotal in the growth of North Hants. South Maitland for a time was known as Rockville because of the large gypsum deposits and the quarries that were established there.

Because of a lack of records, it is impossible to know how much gypsum was mined and traded from the Maitland area in the early years. However, the Department of Mines records that 19,305 tons of plaster were produced at Maitland between 1873 and 1879 with 6,775 tons being produced in 1874 at an approximate value of $6,000 — a considerable sum at that time.

Walton, Hants County, another gypsum boomtown of the time, frequently outproduced the Maitland area and in 1879 produced 3,635 tons.

The net result was that by incredibly good fortune, gypsum brought unexpected wealth to Hants County. Properties thought to be of little value were in great demand. With employment in the quarries came disposable income — actual cash in hand in the form of wages and profits. Population and wealth grew, and the wealth trickled down to almost every sector of society.

Teamsters, loggers and carpenters were required for construction. Millhands, quarrymen, shipbuilders and sailors found paid employment. Wharves had to be built for loading gypsum. Thus began the long climb to prosperity. For with the discovery of gypsum, another even greater industry was born which would put Maitland in touch with the world. The "Mouth of the River" would become one of the leading shipbuilding areas of what is now Canada.

EARLY SHIPBUILDING

The early history of shipbuilding in Nova Scotia is not totally documented. So also with the early vessels of Maitland. We know the Acadians had small coastal vessels, and that they fished and travelled quite extensively in small craft on the Cobequid shore. No complete record of their craft, or of the ships of the early English settlers, is available. So the first man to build a trading vessel in Maitland is probably unknown.

Records and oral history do exist however, even of those early years. Elizabeth Frame notes that:

> Whidden, Frieze, Anderson and Robb and others along the Shore built ships of varied tonnage. Peter Stevens, McDougall, McArthur, and Douglas were among the

> early shipbuilders or shipowners, and run their coasters between the "Mouth of the River" and the Lines, after Graham and Isaac Smith opened the Gypsum quarries at the Rock.[11]

The Whidden family "came from Truro to engage in shipbuilding," Frame notes — one of the earliest specific references to a shipbuilder.[12]

CUSTOM DUTIES

Taxes, even in these early years, were a burden to enterprising traders. Frame notes that there was no port of entry in Douglas and vessels had to enter and clear at Windsor or Parrsboro. Unfortunately, "often a fair wind and tide carried 'plaister' vessels past the Custom House," and "the captain was either unable or unwilling to call, a revenue cutter sometimes followed making an exciting chase."[13]

The implication is, of course, that some may have avoided customs duties. This seems rather unlikely, given the strong religious convictions and church connections of that time.

It would appear from Frame's record that, in the early years of the 1800s, Maitland shipowners had ventured to the West Indies. "Pine timber, lumber, fish and horses, were taken to the West Indies. The returns were meal, flour, salt, leather, iron, dry goods, molasses and," if the usually reliable historian is to believed, "rum."

Yet in a later day, at a ship's launching, the town fathers drove travelling bootleggers from their shores.

NOTES

1. Armour, Charles, Thomas Lackey, *Sailing Ships*, p. 28.
2. Gerald Graham, "Gypsum Trade of Maritime Provinces," *Agricultural History*, vol. 12, no. 3, July 1938, p. 209.
3. *Ibid.*
4. *Ibid.*
5. *Ibid.*, p. 211.
6. *Ibid.*
7. Lawrence, *History of Maitland*, PANS.
8. *Ibid.*
9. *Ibid.*
10. Densmore, Hattie, "Maitland Industry," Halifax *Chronicle-Herald*, August 20, 1963, p. 20.
11. Frame, *Ibid.*, p. 15.
12. McKiel, Rex, East Hants Historical Society, March 13, 1973.
13. Frame, p. 16.
14. *Ibid.*

CHAPTER FIVE

THE GOLDEN AGE OF SAIL

FROM THE early 1800s onward the economy of "Mouth of the River" or Maitland was on an upward spiral. Local and world events as well as men with extraordinary talent created a combination that changed the village into a township and a booming industrial center.

FIRST SHIPBUILDING

Perhaps not the first vessel built in Maitland, but certainly the first vessel of which there is a dependable record, was the *Trial*, launched in 1810. After that time, shipbuilding increased steadily, although the construction was confined to small vessels such as schooners and brigs.

Prominent shipbuilders of the 1830s and 1840s included James Campbell, Jacob Frieze, David Smith and Archibald MacCallum.[1]

David Frieze established a store in Maitland in 1839 and this put him in a key position to engage in trade and shipping.

Communication was frequently with Saint John rather than Halifax, and Cobequid Bay was the most viable route to export gypsum or timber and to import other necessities which might be sold in the area.

THE VISION OF DAVID FRIEZE

Like a prospector who is picking away on a surface lead, unaware of the gold that is just beneath, Frieze probably could not anticipate in the early years how extraordinary circumstances would combine to generate wealth beyond his wildest dreams for Maitland.

Others would capitalize on the initial work done by Frieze, but in the early years he, more than many others, seemed to have the vision to dimly perceive that in the future great opportunities lay ahead.

As so frequently happens, the name of David Frieze is generally unknown in Nova Scotia, and in his own county, except for the writings of local historians. The family name has been lost from the roles and his contribution is largely unrecognized. In my opinion, he was one of the founding fathers of Maitland.

It should be noted then that in 1839, or thereabouts, David Frieze engaged in the shipping of timber to the United States. He combined the triple function of building ships, trading in timber — and possibly gypsum — and the operation of a store to service the growing population.

At that early date, he set a pattern of financial operations that was to prove very successful in the future. Perhaps the work of Frieze was not as glamorous as the swashbuckling captains who followed, but he helped lay the foundation upon which the shipbuilding and trading industry was built.

Frieze was fortunate as well. He was joined in his operations by a very astute partner of Scottish ancestry, Alexander Roy, who had a capacity for business. They established the firm known as Frieze and Roy in the late 1860s. One hundred and thirty years later, the store is still in operation and run by the Roy family. That must tell something of the business capacity of the family.

In the heyday of Frieze and Roy, the *Snow Queen*, a barque

Frieze and Roy Store was established in the 1860s and is still in operation today. The structure was built circa 1839.

of 994 tons, was built in 1872; and the *Trust*, a brigantine of 552 tons, was built in 1876. These ships were operated by the company for over twenty-five years.[2] The vessels, as can be imagined, turned a substantial profit over that long period.

Roy's largest vessel was the *Ester Roy*, built in 1877, a ship of 1,533 tons. Another was the *Alice Roy*, a barque of 610 tons. If the opportunity affords itself and you pass through the quiet village of Maitland, you may see the store still called Frieze and Roy, and may remember something of its history.

UNKNOWN TREASURE — TIMBER

"The vast timber areas of the British colonies in North America were directly responsible for the huge fleet of sailing ships constructed there,"[3] states a foremost authority on sailing ships, Frederick Wallace.

Timber, along with dried fish in some areas, constituted a

principal export for many years. And from Maitland to Noel, good virgin timber was right at the water's edge.

We wonder today how wealthy shipbuilders and traders of Maitland could amass great fortunes and build mansions with furnishings imported from the four corners of the world. The answer is not complicated. They found themselves in unique circumstances. They looked around and discovered green gold — timber — a commodity which the world wanted, and they had in abundance.

The building of simple vessels did not require much financing. The basic material, timber, was at hand and timber also provided a basic commodity for export to start a cash flow.

The east coast of the Maritimes developed the type of man who was skilled with an adze, axe and saw for he carved his own home from the forest. He made furniture, wagons, and sleighs. He was a jack-of-all-trades. He could work iron and build boats to fish on Cobequid Bay. Such men were therefore in the fortunate position of being able to build vessels. They built small ones at first, often hauling out timbers on their backs, then larger ones as profits permitted.

The small vessels were of rough workmanship at first, but the craft developed and was refined with time and experience.

SPRUCE

The men of Hants, like other North Americans, discovered that the humble spruce tree, along with the pine, could be used in shipbuilding. British ships were built of oak, but tight grained spruce would serve and it was there for the taking.[4]

Let us not forget also the precedent of the former residents, the Acadians. They had built vessels a century before Anglo Saxons ever reached these shores. Two small craft were launched at Port Royal by François Grave in 1606. If English settlers were good at working with wood, the Acadians had been masters. The French in Canada had built ships of 120 tons as early as 1660.

Wallace tells of the skill of the French Canadian in woodworking:

> An axe or an adze in the hands of a French Canadian could be made to do wonders. With a broad-axe they could square a log of rough timber as true and as smooth as if it had been sawn and planed, and ... it is said that a Quebec ship carpenter could split a playing card edgewise with his adze.[5]

The skill of the local English woodsman and carpenter was not far behind, for they worked with those tools daily.

THE 1850s — INDUSTRY BLOSSOMS

In later years, Maitland shipbuilders would build massive ships, sail them out of Cobequid Bay, and the vessels would never return. They would build so competitively, so cheaply and of such quality, that shipbuilders found that shipowners throughout the world eagerly sought Maitland ships built of spruce. But in the 1850s, the industry had not yet matured. They were building ships which they operated themselves.

William Dawson Lawrence, whom we shall meet later, built the little barque *Persia* in 1859. It was only 441 tons, but he owned it himself. It cost him £2,600, but in the course of five years she netted Lawrence £10,000 before expenses. In addition, she was sold later for £1,400, for a final profit of £8,800.

Financiers in Halifax began to take notice of the little village and the inhabitants, who seemed to have such a knack of making money. Soon these investors would be pouring money into Maitland, investing in the timber and skills of her

Maitland shipyard crew who built *White Wings*, 1889. Builder, Lockhart Lawrence is in the back row with a white beard and tam.
Maritime Museum of the Atlantic, Neg. no. N3945

woodsmen, shipbuilders and sailors, and making themselves rich in the bargain.

For instance, in the 1860s many Maitland-built ships were owned in Halifax. John Stairs of Halifax played a prominent role. He owned the barque *Fresh Breeze*, 568 tons, built in 1868. During that period, other Halifax owners — Jeremiah Northrup, Robert Boak and Thomas Bayne — owned vessels built in Maitland.[6]

All this created an influx of money and jobs. With jobs came more people and they in turn required services, for those employed would no longer be self-sufficient. Shoemakers, storekeepers, blockmakers and blacksmiths became part of the industrial development that fed on shipbuilding

Miscellaneous Facts

COMMERCE AND INDUSTRY IN MAITLAND

In 1871 the great mapmaker, A.F. Church, created a detailed list of Maitland businesses, tradesmen and clergy:

> J.A. Richie, Trinity Church; J. Curry, Presbyterian; S. Brown, physician and surgeon; A. and C. Putnam, merchants; E. Lynch, stage proprietor (from Maitland to Shubenacadie); J. Monteith, deal, drygoods, groceries; Frieze and Roy, dealers in staple and fancy drygoods, groceries; A.M. Cochrane and son, dealers in drygoods, hardward, cutlery; S.S. Barbrick, dealer in drygoods, groceries, stationery, boots, shoes, medicines, fancy articles; A. Roy, custom house officer and postmaster; J. Trahey, shipbuilder and owner; J. Miller, ship joiner; G. McCulloch, master mariner; J.W. Dwyer, carriage and furniture maker; D.L. McCurdy, carriage maker and blacksmith; J. Drillio, sailmaker; F. Scootney, blockmaker; Wm. Currie, farmer and furrier; T.B.O. Brien, Fishery Comm.; C.J. White, ferryman; Wm. McKenzie, tanner, currier, shoemaker; D. Frieze, J.P.; J. Waddell, master shipbuilder; J. Monteith, calker; Jane O'Brien, teacher; F. McDonald, shoe and boot maker; Adam Roy, Master shipbuilder; A. Putnam, shipbuilder; G. Lattie, farmer; H. McLearn, J.P., general merchant and hotel keeper; N. Dinsmore, manufacturer of lumber and shingles; Isaac McPhee, house and ship joiner; F. Frieze, blacksmith.

A significant event was the arrival of the first physician, Dr. Henry McDowell, a Scotsman "of fine presence, past middle age, whatever his skill might have been as a physician."

Education was always considered important and schools

were built early in the community's development. As time passed, improvements were readily made so that by 1878, the third — a more magnificent school — was completed. Early teachers were Adam Roy, James Bayne and later Reverend Dr. Bayne.

The first minister was Rev. Alexander Dick, who, with his wife Ann Eadie, sailed from Scotland in 1802. He was inducted in a shed used by David Whidden in connection with shipbuilding. This took place on June 21, 1803. Rev. Dick became a very popular preacher.[7]

Rev. Thomas Crowe came from Scotland in 1815 and ministered to the congregation for 54 years.

Mr. Adam Roy Sr. was the first teacher at the Sunday School. An assistant was Miss Eliza Frieze.

The first mail carrier (1832) was Nathan Smith. The role played by these early leaders is important since the family names will appear again and again as Maitland assumes a prominent role in Nova Scotian shipbuilding and trading. The seed of quality leadership and character was sown early in the soil of Maitland and grew rapidly as economic opportunities arose in future.

BANK OPENED

A great benefit to the area was the opening of a new bank in 1873. The Merchant's Bank of Halifax played an important role. Before that time, drafts coming in often had to be taken to Halifax to be cashed. Mr. David Frieze was the first bank manager, and possibly owner, the bank being in what later became Frieze and Roy's store. His son George succeeded him in the post of bank manager.[8]

Shipbuilders often kept large amounts of money at home. One kept $40,000 in his attic for three weeks.[9] The bank remained in operation for over one hundred years, becoming the Royal Bank of Canada.

NOTES

1. Armour, Charles, Thomas Tackie, *Sailing Ships*, p. 90.

2. *Ibid.*

3. Wallace, F.W., *Wooden Ship, Iron Man*, Hodder and Stroughton, London, 1924, p. 6.

4. *Ibid.*, p. 7.

5. *Ibid.*, p. 13.

6. Armour and Tackie, *Wooden Ships and Iron Men*, p. 136.

7. *Ibid.*

8. McKiel, Rex, East Hants Historical Society, March 13, 1972.

9. Densmore, Hattie, Halifax *Chronicle-Herald*, November 28, 1963.

CHAPTER SIX

The Boom Years of Maitland

IT IS DIFFICULT to prove but it is said that in the late 1800s Nova Scotians owned more tonnage of ships per capita than any other nation or region in the world.[1] If nothing else it is an indication of just how important Nova Scotia became during the Golden Age of Sail.

In the boom year of 1874, Nova Scotia had 842 square-riggers on her register, consisting of 104 ships, 300 barks, 9 barquentines, 29 brigs and 384 brigantines, as well as hundreds of "fore and afters."[2]

Nova Scotia shipbuilders received an exemption from municipal assessments for ships under construction to the extent of 50 percent of county rates. This early move by the provincial government was helpful for new builders starting with limited resources.

Nova Scotia ships also were becoming recognized for solid quality. "Spruce frame, juniper and iron knees, with a certain amount of hardwood, made a combination that readily classed A-1 in Bureau Veritas and English Lloyds."[3] This meant a good deal for the sale of ships to foreign countries, and solid construction also affected insurance.

AN EXPLOSION OF WEALTH

Today it is difficult to grasp the magnitude of the flow of capital that came to the town of Maitland during the late 1800s. We are used to relatively slow economic growth or even decline. We believe a community or an industry is growing if it doubles in ten or fifteen years, and are frequently incapable of dealing with the problems, such as increased population, that growth creates.

But consider Maitland. In one summer in her prime, nineteen ships were built.[4] Ships might cost $20,000, when wages were $1.00 per day. During one peak year, Elizabeth Frame estimates that revenue from Hants County ships amounted to nearly one million dollars.[5] If we may estimate that value today, it would probably be the equivalent of more than $20 million in that single year.

1,000 MEN WORKED

"About a thousand men worked in Maitland shipyards in the big summers of that industry. The usual wage was $1.00 per day and board at the yard cookhouse."[6] Consider the economic impact of such a workforce. There would be need for housing, including hotels and boarding houses. Meals would have to be served. Agriculture would be important for fresh milk, cream, butter, vegetables and meat would be needed in great quantities.

The Maitland directory names the many professions involved from harness makers, to teachers. But in shipbuilding alone, there were many trades: dubbers, calkers, fasteners, riggers, joiners and blacksmiths; also carvers who worked on the cabins and imposing figureheads.

The work day started at 7:00 A.M. and ended at 6:00 P.M., with an hour for lunch.

The service industries such as clothing and shoe stores

Maitland School, circa 1928.
Hants East Historical Society

Selma Glee Club under Mr. Ierardi (a blind musician), circa 1915.
Hants East Historical Society

and hardware stores would flourish. There would be a need for a bank to provide for the financial requirements of the shipbuilding industry.

Jobs would be also created in forestry. Hardwood for heat and timber for construction would create work. Milling wood and related work also created jobs and opportunities we can hardly picture in the quiet village of Maitland today.

Real estate would be affected also. More money and more people created demand and property values at that time were higher in constant dollars, I suggest, than they have been since. Maitland was riding a golden tide as powerful as that which roared up Cobequid Bay. She had shrewd leaders who knew how to grasp that opportunity and make it pay — for themselves and for the town of Maitland.

As capital accumulated, wise investments were made. A.A. MacDougall of Selma set up the first shipyard steam mill. The man-powered saw pit cut much timber in earlier years, but it was long, back-breaking work over a ten-hour day.

A large "County Home" was established for the homeless and poor at South Maitland. It closed operation in the late 1960s, but a portion of this large structure still exists today.
Hants East Historical Society

Ship launchings were great occasions with hundreds in attendance with horse-drawn "vehicles with bundles of hay for the horses lashed to the back."[7] These were often great social occasions with a tea, a sale or a dance.

CAPTAINS

A handful of Maitland shipbuilders and captains are remembered, with William D. Lawrence most prominent. Yet scores of prominent captains, with crews of twenty men, traversed the world from England to South America, to San Francisco, to the Orient. Family connections were important and often the shipbuilder had a relation who would be his captain: MacDougall, Roy, Douglas, Putnam, Graham, Lawrence, Howe, Cox, Whidden, Allen, Caddell, Dart, Nelson, McNutt, Walker, Blois, Forbes, McCulloch and MacKenzie were such names, the majority having one or more captains and "one with a dozen."[8]

SHIPYARDS

Shipyards in those boom years included Roy's, at Maitland; a mile south was the Monteith yard. Farther upriver at South Maitland were the yards of William P. Cameron, William McDougall and the Traheys. There was the Archibald MacCallum yard, the Lawrence yard and the Sydney Smith yard. There was the Putnam yard where, in one summer, three ships were launched.

At Selma there was the Alexander A. MacDougall yard from which nineteen barques were launched, and adjoining that were the yards of Pratt and Cox and that of George Oxley Smith.

Down the Cobequid Bay from Selma was the yard of Lorenzo O'Brien at Sterling Brook. At Lower Selma was the yards of James Rose, Charles Cox and Brown and Anthony.

Such activity concentrated in what had previously been scattered agricultural settlements indicates the economic growth and change that took place so rapidly.

THE STAGECOACH

Naturally transportation was needed. The nearest railway in the late 1800s was Shubenacadie, twenty-one miles away. A daily stage left Maitland at 3:00 A.M. in the morning to meet the train in Shubenacadie. The stage returned at noon.

FREIGHT

So much freight came into Maitland that a railway siding was built from the main line at Stewiacke to the Shubenacadie River where Watson's scow and other barges brought it down river to Maitland. Campbell's and Macomber's schooners were Bay freighters along with a small steamer dealing with Saint John, New Brunswick.

Name a modern convenience of the nineteenth century, a means of communication such as the telegraph, and Maitland had it.

TELEGRAPH

In 1872, the Western Union Telegraph Company opened a branch in Maitland and this enabled shipowners and captains to communicate with distant ports of call to which Maitland's ships were then travelling.[9]

PHOTOGRAPHER

A professional photographer operated in Maitland and is responsible for many of the excellent photos that record that great era. His name was Benny Boate (Boak).

BARRISTER

Maitland had a resident barrister to handle the complex legal matters that inevitably arose out of shipbuilding, trading and property transactions. One prominent lawyer was H.T. Harding who was an official of the Maitland Marine Insurance Company.

JUSTICE

George Oxley Smith, Archibald Frame and Robert Barry Eaton were Justices of the Peace and sat in judgement upon the various disturbances, timber contracts and other legal matters.

THE FERRY

A ferry operated from Maitland to Black Rock across the Shubenacadie River from May 1 until November 30. It was mainly for horses and wagons. As early as 1852 it was operated by a Mr. Copeland[10] but it was in the main operated by the Nelson family, although in the busy years, other ferries operated as well.

Some ferries in the early 1900s could carry two cars or several horses and carriages. In these years ferries had engines, but in earlier years used sweeps (oars) and sails among other devices.

In 1924 a scow-type ferry was introduced with an engine. It could carry six motor vehicles. The ferry service ended in 1933 as highway transportation had improved.

In Maitland the ferry left the dock at Cat Street and, weather permitting, travelled to Black Rock, Colchester County, from where it was about a ten-mile journey to Truro.

The economic growth provided by shipbuilding gave importance to the ferry. When that industry subsided, the ferry continued as an important link until rail communication and highways spelled the end.

MAITLAND — A POLITICAL POWERHOUSE

In provincial politics, Maitland, because of its financial and industrial powerbase, became a political powerhouse. The shipbuilding area of North Hants generally had great influence in the Nova Scotia Legislative Assembly.

Prominent politicians were as follows: William O'Brien, MLA, Noel, 1820-1826, 1834-1936; William Lawrence, MLA, Maitland, 1863-1871; William McDougall, MLA, South Maitland, 1871-1874; Alfred Putnam, MLA and MP, Maitland, 1878-1896; Albert Parsons, MLA (Speaker), Walton, 1909-1920, 1925-1933; Hon. Arthur Cochrane, MLA, Maitland, 1859-1863.

Mr. Arthur Cochrane, a local merchant and shipowner, was also in the Legislative Council of Nova Scotia until his death in 1883, and in the Executive Council from 1882 to 1883.

Maitland and the shipbuilding area literally dominated Hants County politics during the above period. This is indicative of the intelligence and industry of the district leaders.

NOTES

1. Truro *Weekly News*, Centennial Edition, June 29, 1967, p. 33a.
2. *Ibid.*
3. *Ibid.*
4. *Ibid.*
5. *Ibid.*
6. *Ibid.*
7. *Ibid.*, p. 48a.
8. *Ibid.*, p. 54a.
9. *Ibid.*
10. PANS, MG100, Vol. 1, 111, #31.

The old Midland Railway Bridge at South Maitland, a major project in its time.

CHAPTER SEVEN

THE RAILWAY TO SOUTH MAITLAND AND THE SHUBENACADIE CANAL

A TOURIST crossing the highway bridge at South Maitland could hardly guess that, at one time, from that point, one might have seen the plume of smoke, the hissing of a steam engine, and heard the click of steel rails as the engine of the Midland Railway puffed its way through the village of South Maitland.

The railway bed still exists as do one or two of the railway-related houses on the old siding. Photos of the time show well-dressed travellers waiting for the trains from Windsor or Truro.

The most costly structure was the first railway bridge across the Shubenacadie River at South Maitland. The old train stopped at such stations as Kennetcook, Upper Kennetcook and Stanley.

The idea of a Windsor to Truro railway originated in 1896 and the line was finally ended about seventy years later. A group of Halifax businessmen obtained a charter to construct a railway to facilitate lumbering, gypsum and agricultural operations. Alfred Putnam of Maitland, shipbuilder and politician, was vice-president of Midland Railway.

In 1897 government aid totaling $618,000 was approved. Building started in 1898 and the line was in operation in

October, 1901. Before the construction of the North Hants High School, many young scholars took this train and attended high school in Windsor.

In 1905 the Dominion Atlantic Railway acquired the company, and then in 1912 leased all interests to Canadian Pacific Railway for 999 years. This train was a local fixture as it shunted its way between Windsor and Truro for over seventy years. But like many other features that North Hants residents knew, it too disappeared. The tracks were lifted and sold, leaving an empty roadbed.[1]

The passenger service ended earlier, but I recall the trains passing through Kennetcook in the mid-1970s.

With the demise of the Midland Railway, another connection with a great and historic past had disappeared forever.

THE SHUBENACADIE CANAL

Another enigma is the Shubenacadie Canal. In today's money it would have cost many millions of dollars. At the northern extremity was, of course, the booming town of Maitland. Maitland provided a link to Cobequid Bay and the Bay of Fundy — and by way of the Shubenacadie River, Grand and other lakes — a transportation link with Dartmouth and Halifax Harbour.

At first it was thought of as a means of rapid movement of troops — a way of getting soldiers from Halifax to the Bay of Fundy in case of American invasion. Later it was seen as a development venture to promote commerce and trade within Nova Scotia.

To many politicians and businessmen of the time, the Canal seemed a golden opportunity. It would aid in development of settlements along its route and would greatly add to the value of land since it would provide a means of transporting timber, agricultural products and manufactured items to markets both in Halifax, the United States and the wider world, through the ports of Maitland and Halifax.

Joseph Howe and others in the 1860s were promoters of railways — not of canals. As with wooden sailing ships, the technology changed and destroyed the economic viability of the Shubenacadie Canal. It was a project which was never fully realized — one that might have helped Maitland when shipbuilding declined. Hundreds of masons labored on the walls of the canals, navvies sweated and battled mosquitoes as they dug the massive excavations with pick, shovel and horse power.

The Shubenacadie Canal essentially followed the old Mi'kmaq route down the Shubenacadie River to Halifax. Contrary to local belief, the Canal actually was completed and, indeed, steam vessels did run along its various courses.

The initial work began in 1826, but the canal company went bankrupt. It was revived as a commercial venture in 1854 under the guidance of Charles William Fairbanks. It began actual operation in 1856 and continued to operate until 1870 when the Intercolonial Railway built bridges that did not allow ships to pass under.

The canal was a costly and labor-intensive project. From Wellington to Halifax there were five locks and two inclined planes, and a total distance of twenty-six kilometers. From Wellington to Maitland was a distance of eighty-nine kilometers and four locks were required. The canoeist today can still see the decaying walls and earthworks in the Shubenacadie River at Enfield and Elmsdale.

Sailboats, rafts, scows and the steamboat *Mayflower* worked the Wellington-Dartmouth end of the Canal. Large quantities of bricks and pottery from the pottery at Enfield were shipped by scow to Dartmouth. Lumber was transported as well. But it all ended in 1870 with the coming of the railway. Again, technology worked against Maitland.

Yet on October 2, 1857, it did not seem so to the fathers of

Maitland as they awaited the arrival of the steamship *Avary* which was the first to navigate the canal all the way from Dartmouth.

A ceremony was arranged and an address given by the fathers of Maitland on that auspicious occasion. It is duly reported in the newspaper, the *Novascotian*, as recorded by the local secretary, Mr. Samuel S. Barbrick:

> To Charles W. Fairbanks, Esq., C.E.
>
> We, the inhabitants of Maitland, beg leave to congratulate you on your arrival at this place with the Steamer, *Avary*. This event we consider will not only be beneficial to this community, but will, we are convinced, tend in future to the welfare and prosperity of Halifax. We think that the time is not far distant when the greater portion of trade that now finds its way to the neighboring province (Saint John, New Brunswick) will pass by this communication to the capital of our own Province.[2]

The congratulatory message was signed by all the important men who attended that great event on that autumn day. W.D. Lawrence was in attendance, as was Adam Roy, Alfred Putnam, Frederick Frieze and David Whidden, and many others. And, while their judgement was correct in most matters of shipbuilding and world trade, their hopes for the canal business were far off the mark, as the Shubenacadie Canal did little for Maitland.

It would be they themselves — the shipbuilders, captains, world traders — who would make Maitland an economic and political force to be reckoned with, not the Halifax backers of the Shubenacadie Canal.

After 1870, the railway was king of transportation and backed by governments. A railway bridge blocked the passage of ships at Enfield. From that point on, the Shubenacadie Canal as a link with Maitland was a dead letter.

Today, as mentioned, many of the old canal works still exist in the Shubenacadie River at Elmsdale and Enfield. Many others nearer to Dartmouth have been restored.

NOTES

1. Report on Hayes Cave, N.S., Department of Mines, 1963.
2. The *Novascotian*, October 2, 1857.

CHAPTER EIGHT

MAITLAND CAPTAINS

AS WE WALK the streets of Maitland, or encounter a massive home in Selma or Noel, we reflect upon the men who a hundred years ago had the means to build such homes. Clearly they were men far different from many work-a-day Nova Scotians of today. Their furnishings were expensive and in good taste, they employed servants, rode in carriages, were educated — not by books, but by travelling, observing and learning throughout the world.

They were adventurers, risk-takers, men with keen minds, capable of making shrewd investments, of managing other men in great numbers on land and sea. They had technical engineering skills to build great ships, and were outstanding seamen, and disciplinarians. They were great men and, as a body, perhaps the greatest Hants County has produced.

But they were not alone in Nova Scotia of that day, for many communities had shipbuilders and wealthy captains. The Bluenose master mariner was well known in the ports of the world. They were world traders, known and respected in South America, the Orient, Great Britain, the United States, and anywhere there was freight to be hauled and money to be made.

Maitland mariners were known for their all-round ability and splendid seamenship. "They had but little polish, but a great deal of ability."[1] Their knowledge was of the practical kind with a minimum of "book-learning."

"Masters who were able to take big ships all over the world without mishap in the old days would fail to pass the British second mate's examination" of the 1920s.[2] Few claimed to be experts in navigation and the majority found their way around the world on the "mere rudiments."[3]

In fact, a great many Maitland master mariners, as well as those from Windsor and Hantsport, owed their initial knowledge of navigation to a very talented and disciplined woman of Maitland, Miss Eliza Frame, who, though small in size compared to the rough men she taught, drilled them in navigation skills and frequently was their only source of academic navigational training.

This remarkable woman — a school teacher, like many others prominent in Maitland's history — has been almost forgotten. It must have been a remarkable sight to see the diminutive woman at the blackboard, in long skirts and wielding a pointer, schooling her husky, bearded students — some of whom would have travelled to the roughest ports in the world — in the rudiments of world navigation.

She taught them well, for history attests that the Maitland masters were some of the finest in the world in their day.

As to practical training, they received the best. They often began seafaring as boys of thirteen or fourteen on local vessels, often captained by relatives or family friends of Maitland and district.

It was a hard school and "only the strong, tough lad could stand it."[4] Master and mates kept them constantly employed in everything related to the upkeep and handling of the ship. And there was no place aboard a Bluenose ship "for a lazy or stupid" boy, or one deficient in stamina or pluck.[5]

Such a "boy" would either "make good" or be out. If he survived he could not help but be proficient for he was drilled in every phase of seamanship. A saucy and mischievous youngster would sometimes get "a rope's ending." He washed and mended his clothes, cared for his personal appearance, and was not allowed to run loose in port.

With such thorough training, the Bluenose sailors were often made second mates at the age of sixteen years. Maitland lads would be no different, especially since they were often related to the captain or owner.

With talent, desire and training, they came ahead fast. In Nova Scotia, youths of twenty could hold the position of first mate, often responsible for managing a difficult and truculent crew. A number were made masters at the age of twenty-two. Despite all the educational facilities of today, it might be hard to find this same degree of responsibility at such a young age.

The North American and Nova Scotian shipmaster was a stickler for discipline. Records of Maitland masters who survived mutiny and shipwreck bear this out. Maritime ships were renowned for cleanliness and smartness of appearance.

In the dangerous conditions of storms, cold and gales, every precaution had to be taken for ship, captain and crew to survive. Lack of discipline, carelessness, slovenliness and disobedience could mean shipwreck and death for all hands. In the heyday of the Maitland masters, they crewed their ships in all ports of the world, often inadvertently bringing dangerous men aboard ship. Therefore stern discipline was often necessary. But there was always good reason, and fairness prevailed.[6]

Still, stories arose about American and Bluenose ships that were often believed, but not always true. Stern discipline and exacting requirements made Bluenose ships the terror of slackers.[7]

Marine historian, F.W. Wallace, sums up the traits which

made the Bluenose master so successful in his day, but would not be accepted today.

> In Bluenose ships, the man who signed on as an Able Seaman or any other rating was assumed to be capable of doing what work the rating called for. And it had to be done according to the highest canons of seamanship. Halfway measures and botch-work would not be tolerated for one minute, while slackness or slovenliness, insolence and "sojering" would be rewarded with such sudden and vigorous punishment that the offender would need skip lively and be tractable if he would remain aboard the ship with a whole skin.[8]

Repugnant as it may sound to us today, discipline aboard sailing ships, and attention to every detail of seamanship, was an absolute necessity in the survival of ship and crew.

Unlike the British naval officer, the Bluenose master mariner wore no uniform. Both master and officers often could not be distinguished from the crew. Everything was business. Show mattered for little. Yet when in foreign port or visiting port officials, as photos show, Maitland captains and others were meticulously and fashionably dressed. Their wives and children, when they accompanied them, were adorned in expensive clothes.

This then was the background and training of the men we shall meet in the following pages. The Maitland master mariner was rough-hewn, astute, tough as leather, courageous and practical. We may look back at these men and wonder at their incredible achievements. We know their provenance, their community background, their rough education and fine families, yet nothing quite explains their amazing achievements or how, after fifty years, that spirit was extinguished and disappeared as quickly as it had arisen.

While the names of many of Maitland's historic figures still survive in Hants County, that of Montieth has vanished from the villages and hamlets of North Hants where the great shipbuilder, Joseph Monteith, was once a powerful, wealthy and influential man. Not a living soul in the area now bears his name.

Joseph Montieth was an unconventional man. His vision of ship design was different from most other North American builders. His ships were easily recognizable for he gave them a unique feature no others had — a stern design strikingly different from any contemporary vessels. None of his ships had the round stern typical of British North American vessels.[9]

Like the great and wealthy William Dawson Lawrence, Montieth had vision, a distinct view of how ships should be built, but also how they should look. The practical Lawrence had a vision of a mighty ship that would employ economy of scale, would be a money-maker and a financial success. Bulk, sturdiness and practicality were concepts close to Lawrence's mind when he designed ships. Historian F.W. Wallace states of the ship *William D. Lawrence*, "I have seen her model and from the look of her I would judge that she was a great ark of a vessel, designed to pack a cargo.[10]

On the other hand, Montieth is said to have built one of the most strikingly beautiful ships ever to have been launched in Canada. "The *Earnscliffe* was called a full-rigged three-skysail yard ship. A more beautiful ship has never been built by any man at any time," said an old seaman.[11] A model of this ship is in the private collection of Mr. Roy Rhyno, Maitland.

This ship, the *Earnscliffe*, was named after the residence of Sir John A. Macdonald, Father of Confederation and Prime Minister of Canada.[12] This we might surmise meant that Montieth was an admirer of the Tory Prime Minister, and was therefore probably a Tory himself. This when many other prominent Maitland shipbuilders were known Liberals.

Montieth was something of a rebel in ship design and politics, and also took artistic pride in the beauty of his ships. He apparently scoffed at superstition and fears of seamen handed down over the years, for he launched the *Earnscliffe*, to the dismay of many, on a Friday the thirteenth.

THE JINX ON THE *EARNSCLIFFE*

As his ship bobbed in the red Cobequid tide, Montieth's hopes were high, for the *Earnscliffe* was indeed a magnificent sight. All who beheld it agreed. It was a large ship, built at great cost. Always a gamble, shipbuilding involved great risk, and sound design counted greatly not just for speed of travel but also in safety. It was not as large as Lawrence's monster ship, but it was a large ship of 1,875 tons and this, combined with the beauty of its design, added to the great occasion of its launching.

As it sailed gracefully out of Cobequid Bay, the best wishes of friends and rivals went with the *Earnscliffe*. Yet even on that exciting day, all did not go well for her. At the launching it appeared that a calamity was in the making, and Montieth must have had second thoughts about his scoffing at superstition. As she reached the water it appeared that the vessel, which was caught by wind and tide, would be grounded on shore. A tug came out but it was not powerful enough to counter the mighty ship. So before the *Earnscliffe*'s career had begun, it encountered trouble.

The signs were not promising, even for a man of Montieth's cast of mind. The vessel was hauled off the muddy shore but, because of the tide and timing, was grounded again in the Bay of Fundy.

Critics might have noted that it was not as sturdy as a Lawrence-built ship or one built by Roy, O'Brien or Frieze, but in general, all seemed well as the great ship sailed into the Atlantic. Sadly, as we frequently learn in the course of life, it is often wiser to choose character and durability over beauty. And so with the *Earnscliffe* for she was to be one of the most troubled ships in Maitland's history. The jinx began on that very first voyage.

THE STRANGE CASE OF ELDRIDGE DENSMORE

Eldridge Densmore was a man accused of meting out brutal treatment on the first voyage of the ship *Earnscliffe.* He was not a particularly tall man, but he was solidly built, muscular with powerful arms and shoulders, and without an ounce of fat. His weight was 200 pounds. His accusers said he had a surly disposition and with his solid build he was formidable when crossed.

Densmore was mate aboard the three-skysail yarder. She was a handsome ship, "and was Maitland's contribution to the large vessels of the last days of Bluenose square-rig."[13]

The *Earnscliffe* was captained by Howard McKenzie, brother-in-law of the builder, Joseph Montieth.

After all these years, the question still remains unsolved. Was Eldridge Densmore an innocent officer trying to keep discipline aboard a ship filled with troublemakers and potential mutineers? Or did he use his size and great strength to terrorize the multinational crew they shipped aboard in Liverpool, England?

The *Earnscliffe* set sail from Maitland to Liverpool, England, with Captain McKenzie in command. It seemed a profitable voyage since McKenzie obtained a 3,000-ton cargo of coal to be loaded from Birkenhead and shipped to San Diego, California.

When in England, it was necessary to add crew members for the long journey across the Atlantic, around the Horn of South America and up to California. Perhaps McKenzie might have been more selective in hiring his crew, but in fact it was not always possible to find ideal sailors in busy ports.

There were sixteen hands in the fo'c'sle, and two boys in the half-deck. There was a mixture of nationalities, one Russian, one Finn, one Frenchman, two Norwegians, three Germans, two Swedes, three Danes, one Irishman and two English.[14] Some had difficulty understanding English, which may have partly caused the trouble.

One great danger on long and difficult voyages was an unstable crew which might mutiny if they felt aggrieved or were led by troublemakers. Captain and mate walked a narrow line in such cases.

One crewman aboard the *Earnscliffe* later complained they were expected to do "a month's work in four days" and said, "we started on what was six months's hell."[15]

It was a long voyage, apparently with a very unhappy and difficult crew. However, Densmore, perhaps with unorthodox methods, managed, through the force of his presence, to keep them in line and finally they reached port in California.

The voyage appeared to be a complete success. Captain McKenzie and Mate Densmore had something yet to learn. Even in 1891 there were shipboard lawyers, and the crew, having failed to master Densmore aboard, sought to best him in court. The charges were as follows: a disgruntled seaman reported years later in the *Liverpool Courier*, England, May, 1925, that "the Mate (Densmore), who was about 200 pounds, and no superfluous flesh, gave an order to the Russian which he did not understand quick enough, so he hauled off and knocked him senseless on the deck."[16] "When we got to San Diego there was not a man without a life mark to remind him he had been in the *Earnscliffe*."[17] The plaintiff also asserted that Densmore had knocked him out with a belaying pin, without provocation. There were other charges as well.

The crewmen took the matter up with the British Consul in San Diego. His verdict was, "Get back to your ship."

Californian lawyers then said they would take the case for half of "what we got." Before the Supreme Court, the lawyers won the case, and Captain McKenzie was forced to pay $350 and the mate $200.

After a hundred years, such a decision would be hard to evaluate. But the author of *In the Wake of Windships*, F.W. Wallace, took the time to visit Maitland many years later and to interview a retired shipmaster concerning the tale. His answer was brief and simple: "No finer man than Captain Howard McKenzie ever trod a deck. Eldridge Densmore was a real mate — one of those who would stand no nonsense, but not a hard man to get along with if a man did right."

So we may never know the correct version of events, but we may surmise that life aboard a sailing vessel in those times was not a Sunday School picnic.

THE WRECK OF THE *EARNSCLIFFE*

The *Earnscliffe* was not favored with good fortune. She was short lived and was lost after less than five years of service. In the mid-90s she rounded the Horn and on a voyage from Cape Town to "Saigon, China," was taken aback by a heavy squall, partially dismasted, and driven ashore on Princess Island. Her bones lay bleached there for many years. F.W. Wallace says she was a magnificent ship and Maitland's contribution to the largest vessels of the last days of sail.[18]

LAUNCHED BY MOONLIGHT — THE *SENATOR*

As in some other areas, ships built in Maitland were frequently completely rigged on the stocks and launched with sails bent and ready for sea. Again Joseph Montieth appears, at least in the historical records, to be a man of a somewhat different cast of mind than his contemporaries.

At midnight and in the eerie glow of moonlight he

launched the big 1,500-ton ship *Senator* in 1878. It was built for Jeremiah Northrup, Halifax.[19]

She had been finished and all ready for launching at high tide, which happened to occur at midnight. To a man like Montieth, a midnight launching did not appear a great obstacle. He hired a tug which was to take the ship down the bay in the dark of night.

But at midnight, there was no sign of the tug. Instead of postponing the launch, as some would have done, Montieth, on the spur of the moment, ordered the ship wedged up, and set the *Senator* afloat.

Luck and good judgement were with him this time, for with "a fair wind blowing as she took to the water, the sails were set and away she went, making a splendid sight with the sheen of the moon on her white cotton canvas."[20] Oldtimers must have shook their heads at Montieth's daring. He was not a man afraid to take a risk. Maitlanders who saw the spectacle as she sailed away would have something to talk about for some time.

MUTINY ABOARD THE *SAVONA*

William P. Cameron of South Maitland built a fine ship, the *Savona*. It was a large vessel of 1,649 tons, and Martin Dickie of Truro was the principal owner. They appointed George W. Stailing to be the first master and he was also part owner.

In 1895 she carried 1,790 tons of shale and 510 tons of tallow from Sydney, New South Wales, to Liverpool. Captain Stailing, aged thirty-two, carried his wife and two boys with him on his voyages, as was a common practice. He was an experienced master, having run away from home at twelve and shipped as a cabin boy. He was a quiet man, but, as some of his crewmen were to discover, "still waters often run deep." Calm and resolute, he was known to act quickly and without fear. Because of dangers presented by shipping unreliable crews, Stailing was known to carry a revolver in his cabin.

F.W. Wallace relates a typical adventure as told to him by one of Stailing's sons:

> We were with father on a voyage from Calcutta to Boston with cargo of Jute, and we had picked up a hard-case crew in India who gave a lot of trouble. One day in the Tropics, my brother and I were listening to mother reading aloud from a book and my father was pacing the poop. There was a large bewiskered Russian Finn going through the motions of caulking a seam in the poop, and my father noticed the way the fellow was 'sojering (loafing) on the job,' and he admonished him. The Fin, in a burst of rage, leaped to his feet and made a swing at father with the caulking-mallet. Had the blow struck home, there is no telling what might have happened, but Dad side-stepped the attack and closed with the Finn, and before we younsters knew it almost, he had the sailor down and groveling on the deck. The man was quickly ironed and kept confined until we reached Boston.

That was not to be the end, however,

> On this voyage, our old Norwegian second mate was assaulted by an Austrian seaman, who made a stab at him with a sheath knife. Wilson caught the blade in his huge calloused hand and snapped it off about half an inch from the handle. The two mixed it up and immediately the ship was seething. A loud voiced Irishman was howling for all hands to down the officers and seize the ship, and things were looking bad.
>
> My brother and I were standing beside mother in the forward companion-way. She was looking out of the window, very much distraught at the scene down on

> the main deck, while we youngsters tugged anxiously at her skirts, filled with curiosity and alarm at what was taking place.

Things had gotten out of hand and the mate rushed to the Captain's cabin. Stailing had been relaxing unaware of the excitement. But when he heard of the mutiny, he was not long acting.

His ship and officers, his wife and family were at the mercy of the dregs of the Calcutta docks. The horrible consequences for his wife and children would not be hard to imagine.

Stailing quietly got to his feet and reaching into the cabinet, retrieved his revolver, probably a forty-five-calibre, common in those days. At close range, no man lives who receives such a bullet in the chest.

Stailing had a way about him, a certain presence, that commanded respect — he was not a man to fool with. The man who crossed him in those circumstances placed himself in danger of losing his life, and the mutineers knew it.

When he reached the deck, his manner and his command did much to restore order. But the black steel revolver held in the hand of a man who would use it assisted also.

"Captain Stailing quickly restored order. The second mate had about fourteen gashes in his head from the stump of the Austrian's knife." Such violent scenes were not unheard of in the golden age of sail.[21]

NOTES

1. Wallace, *Iron Men, Wooden Ships*, p. 161.
2. *Ibid.*, p. 171.
3. *Ibid.*
4. *Ibid.*, p. 161.
5. *Ibid.*
6. *Ibid.*, p. 164-7.
7. *Ibid.*, p. 165.
8. *Ibid.*, p. 167.
9. Wallace, *Windships*, p. 236.
10. *Ibid.*, p. 208.
11. PANS. Misc. Scrapbook #170, p. 273.
12. *Ibid.*
13. *Windships*, p. 236.
14. *Ibid.*, p. 237.
15. *Ibid.*
16. *Ibid.*
17. *Ibid.*
18. *Ibid.*, p. 236.
19. *Ibid.*
20. *Ibid.*
21. *Windships*, p. 243.

CHAPTER NINE

W.D. LAWRENCE AND THE GREAT SHIP

A STORY OF much greater success is that of W.D. Lawrence, shipbuilder, master mariner and politician, who more than any other Maitland captain, achieved fame and fortune and a secure place in Canadian shipbuilding history.

On October 26, 1874, the great three-masted ship, *William D. Lawrence*, was launched. At the time it was said to be one of the largest square-rigged vessels launched in Canada.[1]

One large ship could carry twice the cargo of two small ones, with less crew and fewer operating expenses. This essentially was the idea that prompted Lawrence to build his great ship.

William Lawrence was born July 16, 1817 at Gilford, Banbridge, Northern Ireland, the son of William Dawson and Mary Jane (Lockhart) Lawrence, and immigrated to Nova Scotia as an infant. His parents settled at Five Mile River, near Maitland, when he was still a child.

Lawrence learned the craft of shipwright as a young man in Maitland. He then moved to Dartmouth and worked at Lyle and Chappell's shipyard. He must have realized that few have made fortunes swinging a broad-axe for twelve hours a day in the shipyards of other men. He also pursued a course of studies, which probably were conducted at Dalhousie

W.D. Lawrence as depicted in the Nova Scotia Legislature. His countenance was distinguished by a remarkable, penetrating gaze.

The ship *William D. Lawrence*, 1874.

College. In addition, he studied drafting under Donald MacKay, the great shipbuilder from Shelburne.

Lawrence returned to Maitland and, with slim financial resources, decided to set up his own shipbuilding operation. Thirty pounds was the total capital for his first project. He cut the frames for his first vessel in the woods and carried them out on his back.

The picture of Lawrence as MLA for Hants which hangs in the Nova Scotia Legislature reveals a face hardened with care. But, in his twenties, Lawrence was a large and powerful man, filled with the optimism of youth.

His first ship was the brigantine *St. Lawrence*, a venture which proved successful, and he made a substantial profit with her.

As Lawrence gained mastery over his trade, a series of new vessels slipped from the Lawrence shipyard: the barque *Architect*, the *Persia*, the *W.G. Putnam* and the *Mary*. Lawrence was fifty years old and nearing the height of his building career when he launched the *Pegasus* in 1867.

An excellent picture of what William Lawrence could do in finance and shipping exists in the *Acadian Recorder*, February 21, 1873. Here was an astute businessman of world class, a man who could take calculated risks, and who was to become one of the wealthiest men in Hants County. Yet Maitland had many others of similar capacity.

The *Acadian Recorder* notes: "The ship *Pegasus*, 1,120 tons register, of Maitland, William Lawrence, builder and owner, has been one of the most profitable in this County and province."

From the *Acadian Recorder* report we get a clear idea of the type of world trade and extraordinary financial transactions that Lawrence and other Maitland captains were involved in, and how they earned their substantial fortunes:

> Her first voyage was from Saint John to Liverpool, (England) with deals, then from Liverpool to Boston

> with general cargo, then from Saint John to Liverpool again with deals.
>
> Up to this time she had made nothing, in fact she was behind £900. A quarter of her was owned in England, and the owner there had managed her. Mr. Lawrence now bought the English owner out, and assumed the control of the *Pegasus*. Her first voyage under Mr. Lawrence's management was from Cardiff with a cargo of coal to Yokohama. Her gross freight out was 4,275 pounds. She sailed from Yokohama to the Chinchis Islands in Ballast, and sailed from the Chinchis Islands with a cargo of Guano for Antwerp, gross freight, 6,000 pounds — gross freight on the round(trip) 10,575 pounds, clearing about £7,000.
>
> From Antwerp she went to Cardiff in ballast and loaded with coal for Monte Video, gross freight 2,616 pounds.

The article indicates the *Pegasus* continued to Guanepo, thence to Hamburg, thence to Cardiff, to Hong Kong, and to Ilo Ilo, in the Philippines where she loaded a cargo of sugar for Boston.

These travels took from September, 1868, to December 1872. Each stop added substantially to the Lawrence fortune. During four years and three months, the *Pegasus*, under Lawrence's ownership, had cleared $82,716, paying for herself nearly twice over, "in fact leaving the very comfortable surplus of $35,919."[2]

The article notes that "she has been managed and well handled by her Captain, James Ellis, a son-in-law of Mr. Lawrence."

That $35,919 is difficult to estimate in today's dollars but a shipyard worker earned a dollar a day and today's worker might earn $100 for a ten-hour day. By that rough criterion, the $35,919 would range between $250,000 and $500,000 today — quite a substantial amount.

WAGES

In fact, Charles Armour notes that men's wages ranged from 90¢ to $1.60 per day. Lockhart Lawrence, master builder, was paid between $2.00 and $2.50 per day and William Lawrence himself was paid $4.00 per day. Fifteen thousand two hundred seventy-four man-days were expended in building the *William D. Lawrence.*

In Maitland, one may bring these distant events into present-day reality, since the home of Captain James Ellis still exists, as does that of W.D. Lawrence.

LAWRENCE IN POLITICS

By the 1860s Lawrence was well known in his county and province, and pressure was put upon him to run for the Legislature. Lawrence clearly saw the ruinous consequences of a Nova Scotia deprived of world sea trade in favour of the dubious advantages of economic links with "Upper Canada." He spoke strongly and voted against Confederation. He was MLA from 1863 to 1871.

THE GREAT SHIP

However, this diversion into politics in no way dimmed Lawrence's vision of trade and shipbuilding. After thirty-four years of ship construction, Lawrence hit upon an idea which helped lay the foundation of the Lawrence fortune. The potential economic advantages of a great ship intrigued him.

In September, 1872, in front of his home in Maitland, he laid the keel of the great ship, *William D. Lawrence.* It was larger than anything seen before in Nova Scotia and reached 243 feet in length.

A force of seventy-five men, with his brother Lockhart Lawrence as master builder, worked on the vessel. Operating costs were high. Risking much of his personal wealth in one great gamble, Lawrence borrowed heavily.

The ship had three decks, and weighed 3,400 tons. Two hundred tons of bolts were used in her construction. The main mast measured 200 feet and the main yard ninety feet. Eight thousand square yards of sail were used to propel her.

In his records Lawrence notes his annoyance with the many critics who attempted to discourage him, critics from the United States, England and Europe. Finally his patience wore thin and he wrote:

> But on one occasion I had to act differently. A certain man came into my shipyard and, before bidding good-day, began to find fault with the ship. He said everything about the ship was wrong. It would be impossible to make her sea-worthy. She would ruin me and everyone else who had anything to do with her. I tried to reason with him but to no purpose. At last I said to him, "Friend, do you know the way you came into this yard?" He said, "I think I do." "Then, sir, please take your back tracks, and if you need any assistance, it is handy." He took his departure and never came into the yard again.

The period of construction lasted from September, 1872, until October, 1874. The announcement that the *William D. Lawrence* was to be launched on October 27, created a flurry of excitement.

Ships' launchings, even for smaller ships, meant a day's celebration. A launching was always filled with suspense and even more so with Lawrence's "risky" venture. Such a giant vessel might not leave the ways; it might capsize; or worse, it might mire in Cobequid mud.

4,000 VISITORS

Four thousand visitors came to view the proceedings, many from Halifax, Parrsboro, Windsor and the villages of Hants County. At one o'clock the work force wedged up the ship for launching.

The vessel, with 400 tons of stone for ballast, weighed 3,800 tons. Half an hour passed. Despite the constant hammering of carpenters and workers and Lawrence's busy directions, the ship sat immobile like a great idol, with eight thousand eyes riveted upon her. The critics must have enjoyed those moments.

Then at ten minutes to two, the monstrous vessel vibrated, then moved slightly on the greased slips. A sigh went up as the ship gathered momentum, careening toward the brown waters of the bay. Supports crashed aside as the ship thundered seaward.

The hush of suspense ended as the waters parted under the ship's great weight and she glided into the full tide of the Fundy. The first hurdle of Lawrence's massive financial venture had been cleared. Out on the bay the leviathan floated placidly. The launching was a success but greater tests lay ahead. Could the great ship stand the battering of the Atlantic? Could the massive debt it incurred be paid off?

Lawrence was soon to prove his confidence was not unfounded. On November 15, he left Maitland for Saint John with the ship under the command of his son-in-law, Captain James Ellis. Deals were loaded there and in twenty-three days, the vessel was in Liverpool, England. Lawrence then loaded coal at Birkenhead and set sail for Aden.

On the morning of June 7, 1875, the great ship encountered a gale that damaged a mast and delayed her arrival until August. Lawrence took a steamer to Bombay to purchase new spars, a lengthy trip across the Arabian Sea.

He returned, made repairs and, on September 13, the vessel and her enterprising master set sail for Callao, Peru.

A GREAT MAN MAKES A GREAT MISTAKE

In depicting W.D. Lawrence, we tend to paint a picture of a man who never made a mistake. However, a seldom-told story exists in which Lawrence, either by impatience or daring, made a blunder that had serious consequences, and could have been ruinous. He was, however, one of those fortunate individuals who seemed to survive the most disastrous circumstance.

Historian F.M. Wallace records such an incident. He notes that the only way the great ship, *William D. Lawrence* would make fast passages was "with the wind aft and the skipper cracking on (sail)." During the initial voyages, Lawrence himself sailed on board, with Captain Ellis officially in charge of the ship.

Ellis was a cautious man, but Lawrence was "exceedingly anxious to see what she could do when given a chance, and on her first or second voyage, guano-laden and bound for Europe ... she was running with a stiff breeze astern and logging fifteen knots under a press of sail."[3]

Captain Ellis became concerned, since to him the strain on the masts was becoming great, and he wanted to reduce some of her canvas, but his father-in-law and boss, W.D. Lawrence said, "Hold on a bit until the log reads sixteen knots. She'll make it."

W.D. Lawrence was then a man of at least fifty-seven years. Yet he still had the same nerve and risk-taking capacity that brought him to his position of power and influence. But this time, he had gone too far. His famous luck had run out.

Ellis was in no position to disobey his father-in-law's command, so he held steady listening to the great ship groan under the strain, while Lawrence, with a high wind and ever bulging canvas, tried to push her to sixteen knots.

A few tense minutes passed as Captain Ellis watched anxiously. Then the ship dove into a "big sea and fetching up, the three topmasts, topgallant-masts, and yards went over the side — a beautiful mess."[4] One can picture the incident. The big ship storming along through the high rolling gray-beards of the Southern Ocean at a fifteen-knot clip and the tall spars pitching over into the sea with a thundering crash when she fetched up on the back of a huge surge.

But with Lawrence's ingenuity, he managed to salvage the voyage and come out still ahead. Yet, the incident demonstrates that even the greatest of men, a master mariner, can be too confident and go too far.

A pleasant journey of eighty days followed. Lawrence crossed the Indian Ocean, passed Australia, and sailed across the South Pacific. He arrived in Peru on December 3.

A year before he had signed a contract to carry guano, a valuable fertilizer, from Pabellon de Pica, Peru to Havre, France. When he arrived in Peru, the price of guano had fallen and the French firm, Dreyfus Freres and Cie, attempted to break the contract. The company refused to load. Other ships' masters became discouraged and sought cargo elsewhere.

Lawrence took a different view. He was a hard-nosed businessman as well as a shipbuilder, and he had bills to pay. A charter had been signed which was binding and demurrage could be collected as a penalty for keeping ships waiting. Not by seamanship or even by shipbuilding — but by business acumen — was Lawrence's fortune built.

Had his nerve failed, he might have received nothing. Lawrence waited, anchored at Pabillion de Pica, quietly building up demurrage charges. He waited eleven months. Finally Dreyfus, in exasperation, decided to load the giant ship.

But they had not fully appreciated the tenacity of the man from Maitland. When Lawrence reached France, he hired an attorney and, when he finally got the French company through the High Court of Rouen, Lawrence received

Captain James Ellis, captain of the ship, *William D. Lawrence.* His grand home still stands near Maitland.
Maritime Museum of the Atlantic, Neg. no. N3875

£10,620 for demurrage and interest. This, added to the freight charges on the guano, totalled £23,000 pounds, a magnificent sum in those days. In one world voyage, climaxed by a wise legal move, Lawrence had added substantially to his wealth.

Lawrence finally returned to Halifax in June of 1877 when he was seen calling upon his creditors in his shirt-sleeves, carrying a red bandana full of guineas and paying off his debts. The *William D. Lawrence* had left Nova Scotia with a debt of $27,000 which was almost totally paid in a single voyage.[5]

The critics had been wrong, indeed. The great ship made an annual return on the original investment of 20 percent in the eight years Lawrence owned her. He finally sold the ship to a Norwegian company for $140,848. The name was changed to *Kommander Swend Foyd*, and she remained afloat for another sixteen years.

Lawrence had built a grand home at Maitland, also on a large scale. It still exists as a provincial museum.

A little-known character is Captain William Lawrence Jr., who took command of the great ship later on. He was "a hard-driving Bluenose skipper and is said to have made the best passages in her. He made a round trip a month sooner than Captain Ellis and by this earned an extra $1000 for his father, "who was so pleased he gave him the money as a present." On that trip Lawrence Jr. drove her like a "madman, cracking on and carrying sail until he had his crew scared stiff."[6]

The *Acadian Recorder* noted on February 21, 1873 that the *William D. Lawrence* was to be "the largest vessel ever placed upon the blocks in the Dominion or in British America."

Other Lawrence ships were also successful. The record of operations with the *Pegasus* had been equally notable.

His record with his barque *Persia* was the same. Launched in 1869, she cleared £8,800 during five years of operation.[7]

To get an idea of the financial boom that took place in Maitland at the time, the *Acadia Record* of February 21, 1873, paints a scene of bustling shipbuilding activity: "James Trahey of Five Mile River has two ships in the stocks, one a barque of about 800 tons." He also had another in progress of about 1,100 tons. James MacDougall of Five Mile River and William MacDougall both had large vessels under construction. Frederick Putnam of Maitland and David Pratt of Upper Selma both had large ships under construction. Also building or getting the timbers out of the forest to build were Captain Alexander MacDougall, Captain Charles Cox, Lorenzo O'Brien and Andrew Anthony. At Rockville, Captain James MacDougall was getting out timber for a brigantine.

The *Recorder* noted that, "There will probably be more vessels built in the Maitland district this year, (1873) than ever before. The whole registered tonnage ... will probably amount to nearly 10,000 tons."[8]

Thus Maitland and district had reached its peak. It had

made its mark in Canada's shipbuilding industry. Good times still lay ahead but the following decades saw a slow decline. By that time, however, the names of Lawrence, Roy, Frieze, O'Brien, Anthony, MacDougall, Cox, Montieth and others were already the stuff of legends, firmly rooted in the shipbuilding history of Canada.

REMARKS AND WRITINGS OF W.D. LAWRENCE, MLA

W.D. Lawrence, House of Assembly, 1868, Resolution Relative to the Repeal of the British North America Act.

> ...I have confidence in the integrity and capacity of the people of Nova Scotia to govern themselves as in days gone by. I love the good old flag of England; I was born under it, and I hope to die under it. But I have no desire to live under Canadian rule; I love freedom too well for that. ...No sir, the people of Nova Scotia know their rights, and will never submit to be kept in leading strings by Canadians. ...Look at the outrageous tariffs the Canadians have forced upon us, and what do we get in return ... We now pay one third more tariff than we formerly paid and receive nothing in return.
>
> (Of Joseph Howe.) I confess sir, that I was shocked at some latter day conversions — conversions that seemed to take place almost in the twinkling of an eye. Such movements of the affections ... seem a little out of nature. When we see old political enemies, abusing each other in all that is vindictive and malicious, and suddenly falling in love with each other, it cannot fail to make a deep impression on the public mind.
>
> The people of this country, want nothing else but fair play, and the government that tries to force any thing else upon them will only be sowing the wind to reap the whirlwind. Sir, this Confederation with Canada was

> conceived in sin and brought forth in iniquity. ...It is well known that the self appointed delegates misrepresented the sentiments of the people of Nova Scotia...
>
> I have spoken out freely what I have felt it my duty to say. ...We must look the dangers which threaten us in the face.

Election Speech, Windsor, N.S., on nomination day 1871:

> But sir, who can we trust? What can we expect when we see a man like the Hon. Joseph Howe go over and join the enemy?
>
> Hear him in this very town in 1867, he said, "Take a Nova Scotian to Ottawa, freeze him up for seven months in the year where he cannot see the mast of a ship or smell salt water, and he will die of despondency, and no Nova Scotian who has not an axe to grind will ever go there a second time." Alas, poor human nature what has changed the Climate at Ottawa within so short a time. Simply a "sallary" of $5,000 per year.

On candidates:

> A representative of the people is considered public property, and is often held up as a public target to be shot at; and like the scapegoat of old, have to bear all the sins of the people ... I have served you eight years and have never surrendered my own convictions to the will of others, but have tried to maintain a steady adherence to truth, whether in favor or out of favor. My aim has been to do the best I could for the interest of the county ... And sir, while working for the interest of Hants County, I believe in working for the interests of the whole country as well, because a man serves his party best who serves his country best...(William D. Lawrence was defeated on election day, 1871)

Lawrence was attacked (December 1883, *Acadian Recorder*) on the viability of building a large ship, and that one would be hard to handle. He answers:

> Vessels that (small) size undoubtedly would be best for men of small ideas, and who are too small calibre to handle large ships, and have therefore to play a smaller game. ...Capt. Ellis worked the *William D. Lawrence* as easily as a pilot boat ... and handled her like a yacht.

To T.C. Jones, January 14, 1868.

> The new Canadian Government has raised our tariff from ten to fifteen percent, and many of the union men are now kicking hard against it. There is nothing brings men to their senses so quick as to put your hand into their pocket. Our 19 men that went to represent Nova Scotia at Canada, had no more influence there than 19 grasshoppers. All Canada was as one man, and if a member from the maritime provinces said anything in opposition to the policy of the government, he was snubbed, even though he were a supporter.

Letter to Isaac Sanford, February 20, 1869:

> Tupper and Archibald forged out the chains to bind us to Canada and Joseph Howe undertook to clinch them. You will find no deserter in me. I will stick to the course of the people and if I fall, I will fall with the people.

Letter to Captain Ellis, May 13, 1869:

> Joe Howe has sold himself to Canada, for a "sallery" of $5,000 per year, and has moved up to Canada bag and baggage. There is a very strong feeling growing in

Nova Scotia in favor of annexation to the United States.

* * * * * * * * * *

When we read the journals and speeches of W.D. Lawrence, we can see that he was far more than a shipbuilder, architect and businessman. In his clash with Joseph Howe, we see a man of intelligence, wit, foresight, patriotism, conviction and, most of all, sound judgement.

In the great debate on the economic effects of confederation with Canada and review Nova Scotia's decline, we may ask, who was right, Joe Howe, or William D. Lawrence?

NOTES

1. Charles Armour notes that the *William D. Lawrence* was the largest ship built in the Maritimes, but she was only slightly larger than the *Morning Light*, built by William and Richard Wright, Saint John, in 1855. And she was not the largest square-rigged ship built in British North America. The largest was *Baron of Renfrew*, of 5,294 tons, built by Charles Wood on the Island of Orleans, Quebec, in 1825. Her dimensions were 304 feet 1 inch, breadth 61 feet, and 5,294 tons.
2. *Acadian Recorder*, February 21, 1873.
3. Wallace, *Wooden Ships, Iron Men*, p. 208.
4. *Ibid.*
5. Hawkins, W.J., *Atlantic Advocate*, "Wm. Lawrence and the Great Ship," March 1981, p. 21. (based on the original work by Archibald McMechan).
6. Wallace, *Windships*, p. 209.
7. *Ibid.*
8. *Ibid.*

CHAPTER TEN

CAPTAINS PUTNAM AND SMITH

CAPTAIN WILLIAM PUTNAM — THE SAIL-DRAGGER

Apart from Joseph Montieth and Eldridge Densmore, one of the most colourful figures of Maitland was Captain William Putnam, who had the reputation of being a great "sail-dragger." Frederick Wallace recounts a tale of when Putnam was a young captain. He was bound from Cow Bay, Nova Scotia, for Boston, commanding the ship *Nancy* with a cargo of coal. The brig suddenly foundered one stormy night and all hands were drowned except Captain Putnam, who clung to a ladder for forty-eight hours before being rescued. It was thought he was driving the vessel so hard she opened up.[1]

Another story of Captain Putnam's sail carrying was while he was commanding the Maitland barque *Edward Burrow* and was bound south across the Bay of Biscay from Cardiff. It was blowing a gale and he had given orders to clew up the main-topgallant-sail. The men whom he sent aloft were a long time on the yard and apparently could not muzzle it. A somewhat impatient man, Captain Putnam watched their efforts for a while and then finally said to the mate, "Call 'em down, Mister, and set it again." If they could not or would not do the

This is the former home of Captain William Putnam, the "sail-dragger", as seen today in disrepair. It was built circa 1850-1860.

job, then Putnam would let them take the consequences. He did not lack courage or bravado, and if not obeyed, he would not worry and was prepared to defy the elements.[2]

While in command of the *Sovereign* in 1879, a large vessel of 1,192 tons, he again showed his devil-may-care attitude, and love of speed and full sail. He made the passage from Portland, Me., to Liverpool, England in December in the brief time of eighteen days. It is also claimed that the *Sovereign*, while under Putnam's command, made the fastest passage on record from San Francisco to Copenhagen.[3]

Putnam was master of this vessel for many years until she was sunk in collision with a steamer in the early 1890s.[4] His large home still exists in Maitland, though vacant and badly in need of repair.

THE BAD LUCK OF CAPTAIN CHARLES D. SMITH

In any endeavor, no matter how great or small, good fortune plays a role. One of the traits the Emperor Napoleon demanded in his marshalls was that they must possess "good luck." Often the fate of a man's career, a battle or the survival of a nation, depends on sudden and unpredictable events. Bad luck has destroyed many talented and deserving leaders of men.

Thus it was with Captain Charles Smith. He had been a most successful shipmaster with a very good record for quick passages and profitable voyages. He then undertook to command a barque, *Erinna*, 1,125 tons, built in Selma, in 1877.

There Captain Smith's good fortune ended. There appeared to be something sinister and evil about the *Erinna*. In Smith's seven years command of her, tragedy followed tragedy, each incident taking its toll upon Smith, who unlike his fellow Maitland captain, William Putnam, took things "personal" and over seven grueling years in command of the "sinister" vessel, the tragic and unexplained events weighed heavily on his mind.

Brown and Anthony had built the ship, and nothing seemed amiss at her launching at what is now Anthony Park, Selma. Yet under Smith's command in the first years, four men were washed overboard. At another time four more died of smallpox. Charles Smith was apparently a sensitive man, and perhaps began to blame himself for the tragedy he was bringing upon his men and their families. He and his ship were creating many widows and orphans.

As time passed more deaths occurred. Most were single deaths. Some were drowned, some were killed and some simply died aboard the ill-fated *Erinna*.

On February 3, 1885, on a voyage from New York to Antwerp, the *Erinna* played the final most devastating card.

The accursed ship foundered in mid-Atlantic and sank beneath Captain Smith's feet, leaving captain and crew stranded at the mercy of the elements half-way between America and Europe in the dead of winter.[5]

Ironically, Captain Smith again survived, and again only one man was lost. But looking back, it seems this final blow was too much for Smith. In all, twenty-two men had lost their lives on the ship *Erinna* while under his command, yet he himself still survived.

One would think that with the sinking of the *Erinna*, the fatal relationship between Captain Smith and the ship was at an end. This was not so. *Erinna* was not yet finished with the unfortunate Smith. Memories of the terrible deaths continued to haunt him. Even after the ship had gone to the bottom of the sea, she did not release him from her grasp.

F.W. Wallace, in reporting this sad tale, relates that: "All these happenings had such an effect upon Captain Smith that he lost his mind and eventually died in an asylum."[6]

NOTES

1. F. Wallace, *In the Wake of Windships*, p. 242.
2. *Ibid.*, p. 243.
3. *Ibid.*
4. *Ibid.*
5. *Ibid.*, p. 249.

CHAPTER ELEVEN

THE *MILTON*: ORDEAL BY SEA

ON AUGUST 9, 1881, the *Milton* loaded coal at Shields, England, destined for San Francisco. Full-rigged and a large vessel of 1,400 tons, she had been built by Brown and Anthony in 1879 and launched at the site of what is now known as Anthony Park.[1]

The captain was Henry MacArthur. In earlier years, that surname appears in the lists of Col. Small's 84th Regiment. He was not a tall man, but powerfully built, though somewhat debilitated by rheumatism. Records show he had a cast in his right eye. He was recognized for his strength of character.

On a previous occasion his vessel had become water-logged in the north Atlantic and he had clung to the rigging and survived. His next sea adventure on the *Milton* was to test that luck again.[2]

His wife was Kate MacArthur, also born in Maitland. Archibald MacMechan tells us that she was no ordinary woman, that she was strong in mind and body, fair of face, educated, musical, observant and a devoted wife and mother.

She lived for over two years on the vessel. The ship was her home and nursery for, on the world-straddling journeys, she took her two sons with her — Archie, four and Frankie, two.

The ill-fated voyage was blessed with good officers —

Charles Carroll of Windsor, N.S., first mate; and Edwin S. Anthony, Maitland, second mate. Anthony was only eighteen but had spent five years at sea. Many of the crew of seventeen, as time would prove, did not always live up to the standards set by these men. Another man from Hants was a loyal seaman named Ettinger.

The *Milton* was a fine and large ship, and the voyage across the Atlantic, around the Horn and into the South Pacific, was blessed by fair winds and good weather. "Day by day the big ship ploughed her stately way across the vast, empty sea," and with an able, if ailing captain in command, she had sailed three quarters of the voyage.[2]

Yet the voyage was a long one, almost straddling half the globe — not uncommon for Maitland ships of the day. They had been at sea almost five months, and just north of the equator on December 22, 1881, when smoke began to rise from the main hatch. The equatorial heat and dampness may have been factors assisting spontaneous combustion of the cargo of coal.

MacArthur had been confined to bed. His rheumatism was severe and he was "hardly able to move a finger." This sick man was faced with the challenge of saving the ship and his family and crew — fire in mid-ocean was a terrible disaster.

His wife helped him dress and he forced himself to the deck and took command of pumps and bucket brigade. They fought the growing fire all afternoon and into the night, but beneath their feet they felt the heat growing in intensity, and the possibility of a massive explosion was always a threat.

MacARTHUR ABANDONS SHIP

In the darkness of mid-ocean at 3:00 A.M. on December 23, they lowered three lifeboats to escape. The hold was an inferno and any hope of saving the ship was gone. Two days before Christmas, Kate MacArthur found herself and her children amid the swells in an open boat. Safety and their destination was 1,200 miles due north at Cape St. Lucas, California.

Maitland captains were known for their discipline and iron will, but they were also known for their skill in seamanship. MacArthur was to prove himself a master mariner.

Into his twenty-four-foot vessel he packed every necessity that he could salvage from the burning hulk, which now glowed like a massive torch on the dark Pacific. Canned food, water, blankets, compass, navigation gear — nothing was forgotten by the clear-headed master. There might be an early rescue, but MacArthur prepared for the long haul. It was a wise decision.

The captain's boat led, followed by second mate Anthony's and in the rear was first mate Carroll's. They followed stern lights. On Christmas Eve, Carroll's boat was seen, but at dawn it had disappeared in the darkness, not to be seen again. Christmas day was spent searching in vain, and the little flotilla pressed onward.

The small vessels often shipped water in the heavy seas and blankets and clothes were soaked. "The heat of morning would draw a thick white steam from the bedding and it soon rotted."[3]

It was on the ninth day adrift that Anthony discovered, on awakening, that the seaman on watch had lost sight of the Captain's sternlight during the night. So another boat was separated. Anthony, a very capable seaman, crowded on more sail and, by luck, managed to overtake Captain MacArthur and was ordered to join the Captain for the night. The next morning the second craft was lost again and so the Captain's vessel forged on alone.

Luckily on the twenty-third day, the second boat was picked up by a British ship, *Cochin*, and was saved. By this time the Captain's boat was far away, still heading toward

California, with MacArthur, assisted by Anthony, navigating the equatorial current and counter currents, and beating against the northeast trade winds.

TREACHEROUS CREWMEN

The struggling voyagers were now well into the new year, but on January 4, 1882, MacArthur discovered treachery among the crewmen aboard the boat. He had trusted them but, while he slept at night, the crew had been drinking the rationed water and worse, had punctured canned tomatoes and drunk off the fluid. To deceive him, they had replaced the tins in which the tomatoes were rotting in the heat.

MacArthur and Anthony then had to remain on watch all night to secure water and food supplies which were running low. Despite the suicidal conduct of his men, MacArthur divided the supplies daily, share and share alike, for man, woman and child.

MacMechan depicts him at this point as "a sunburnt, bearded figure with bloodshot eyes steering his big boat northward, ever northward, with his revolver ready to his hand. Under the rude awning are his wife and children and forward the cowed and treacherous foreigners."

A STRANGE VESSEL

Suddenly MacArthur thought his luck had changed. Six miles to the north he spotted a strange vessel. He came about to meet the stranger's path. With heavy seas and little wind, he ordered the treacherous crew to the oars, and to encourage them, dispensed two gallons of the remaining water. They waved — they shouted for deliverance. But to no avail. A squall settled on the water and the ship disappeared, never to be seen again. All that resulted was the loss of two gallons of precious water.

MacArthur's log reveals that on January 18, the last drop of water was gone. He was now faced with a new challenge — death from lack of water. As Samuel Taylor Coleridge put it, "Water, water everywhere, nor any drop to drink." Other men might have given up, as did some of the crew. But MacArthur was not such a man. Remarkably the tougher conditions became — the lack of water, the heat, the disappointment — the stronger he became. The formerly healthy men lay at the bottom of the boat, while the invalid, MacArthur, with one hand on the tiller and the other on his revolver, charted his course northward. Skin and bones, eyes bloodshot and infected, his iron will prevailed.

Kate MacArthur records her suffering:

> My tongue got thick, and stuck out between my cracked lips, and I seemed burning for water. I used to get a little relief by binding my head and throat with cloths dipped in the sea, but still the thirst kept raging worse and worse ... As I lay in the bottom of the boat with the little sufferers (her children), and heard the swish of the sea against the side, the memory of every drink I had ever enjoyed came back to tantalize me...

But ingenuity and inventiveness was also a trait of the Maitland sailors. MacArthur or Anthony had heard of evaporating salt water and condensing it into fresh water by the use of containers, tubes and a fire. From tins they fashioned a condenser and, chipping at the innards of the boat, found enough wood for a fire. In this way, they staved off death. They made almost a quart of water in twenty-four hours. The process was only limited by the wood that could be spared from the boat's thwarts and gunwales.

The journey proceeded. MacArthur kept the boat on course. Each received a mouthful of water every twenty-four hours.

CREW MUTINIES

A crewman, perhaps crazed with lack of food and water, crept forward during the night, seeking to steal water. Anthony was at the tiller and nudged the captain with his foot. MacArthur acted swiftly and leveled a deadly blow with a club knocking the seaman low. He was found to be carrying a "vicious looking knife." Ironically, the blow which knocked him out was an act of kindness for he was the only sailor to survive.

Strange as it may seem, though most on board were near death, without question the strongest surviving was MacArthur who had risen from a sick bed over forty days before.

BABY DIES

The first on board to die was the youngest. Kate MacArthur recorded later: "My little boys began to cry for water. My two-year-old baby Frankie lay moaning out of his parched mouth, and died in my lap of hunger and thirst. It was too much ... too much." That was on February 2.

Mrs. MacArthur would not allow her son's body to be buried at sea. Sharks continued to encircle the boat and she would not allow him to be eaten. He was wrapped in canvas and placed in a tin box to receive a Christian burial, if they ever reached land.

Unknown to most, Kate MacArthur had denied herself food for the sake of her children, giving them much of her share. She had hoarded a portion of hard biscuit for two weeks for her last child.

The second death came on February 5. Ole Johansen, an older man and ship's carpenter, died.

Shortly after daylight on February 6, MacArthur sighted land. It was St. Roque Island, approximately five hundred miles north of Cape St. Lucas, California. Captain MacArthur had performed a remarkable feat. He had travelled 2,619 miles in an open longboat, despite difficult winds and currents. The desperate company had been at sea in gales, in blazing sunlight, in cold and in heat. Hunger, seasickness, dehydration, continued disappointments, mutiny and even death had not broken Henry MacArthur's iron will. Apart from that, the feat of navigation, particularly since his eyes had been strained and infected from continuous use of the sextant, was remarkable.

MacArthur in early February was the only man fit for duty. Edwin Anthony was weak from hunger and thirst and the three remaining sailors "mere skin and bone, were lying helpless in the bottom of the boat."

Deliverance, however, was not yet at hand. St. Roque Island is merely a small barren rock, far removed from California. It would supply little water or food even if a landing had been possible. MacArthur with his crew of invalids and dying men was forced to press onward. But it was doubtful if they could make the remaining five hundred-mile journey.

ANOTHER VESSEL

As evening fell new hope was raised. They spotted another vessel to the east about five miles. Mustering his last energy he tried to reach the schooner and signal it.

Night closed in and the sail disappeared, and with it all hope of rescue. That broke Kate MacArthur's will to live; she urged her husband to end the terrible agony by pulling the plug from the bottom of the boat. "We will wait a little longer," MacArthur responded.

The wind had died. MacArthur waited in the darkness, listening and straining his bloodshot eyes for even a shadow of the vanished sail. In the remote distance he thought he saw it again. Then it became clearer. It was in fact the schooner. They had both been becalmed and by miraculous good fortune she had come closer to their boat.

Now was the time for supreme effort. They must reach the schooner or perish. MacArthur had the will to "set his living skeletons rowing the longboat towards the schooner."

For sixty minutes the ghostly crew toiled at the oars, shouting, waving to gain the attention of the schooner. For some, their dying strength went into the struggle to gain the distance which would secure their deliverance.

Standing in the stern, MacArthur shouted, "I have lost my ship and have been cast away for forty-six days in the boat. We are perishing for water and food."

The schooner captain had seen them and flung a line, by which the crew of skeletons was drawn alongside. Kate and her husband thought that rescue was finally at hand. But the schooner then slackened the line and, rather than providing assistance, let them drift astern.

The wind rose, the schooner's sails filled and MacArthur found himself towed forty feet in the schooner's wake. More treachery. More evil fortune. What hope that was left aboard this miserable boat was dashed when the Spanish captain cut the line and fired a gun as his ship sailed ahead leaving MacArthur and his crew drifting helplessly. This final cruel and sadistic blow was more than reason could comprehend.

They drifted for an hour. Then, near midnight, two men appeared rowing a skiff, carrying a beaker of water. Their actions seemed friendly, so Kate MacArthur and her son got into the skiff and were rowed away into the darkness.

Mrs. MacArthur's condition was obvious to the Spanish captain. As well as suffering from starvation and thirst, she was also well along in pregnancy.

The schooner was the *Thor*, and the captain a Spaniard, Chirstobal Sosa, with a Mexican crew. Kate MacArthur's Spanish was good enough to let the captain know that they were not pirates as he had feared, but shipwrecked seamen dying of thirst and hunger.

ONE MORE DEATH

The Spaniard sent out the skiff once again. Captain MacArthur, Edwin Anthony, young Ettinger and seamen Tilly Anderson and Annesitt were brought aboard the *Thor.* Rations were meager but the Spanish captain and the Mexicans were generous with what they had — mostly black bread.

Having exhausted the last reserves of his strength, MacArthur finally, after forty-six days of constant strain, lay down and fell into a deep sleep. He had warned his men against drinking large amounts of water in their worn condition. The Nova Scotians heeded his warning, but Tilly Anderson secretly crawled to the water cask, twisted out the bung, and drank without restraint. Despite all efforts, he died on February 7, 1880.

On February 9, they spotted the smoke of a steamer, *Newbern.* MacArthur again boarded his boat and transferred all hands to the American passenger ship bound for California.

A BIRTH AND A DEATH

Seamen Annesett and Ettinger were so weak they could not rise from the bottom of the small craft. Captain Thomas Huntington received them all with every kindness and assistance. Despite this, seaman Ettinger died within a day. Captain MacArthur and his son Archie were in the best condition and Edwin Anthony and Kate MacArthur could get up the side of the American ship without assistance.

As she came aboard Mrs. MacArthur heard a passenger exclaim, "Oh! look at the poor squaw, so black and weather-beaten."

Yet another event lay in store before their eventual arrival on land — this time a happy one. On February 16, as the *Newbern* was entering the harbour at Guyamas, Mrs. MacArthur's baby was born. It weighed only three pounds, and yet as MacMechan tells us in the 1920s, "the boy grew to manhood and is now a distinguished physician in California." He was named "Newbern" — Newbern MacArthur.

Henry MacArthur did not escape without some injury. His eye became inflamed from constant sunlight and use of the sextant. An oculist had to perform a delicate operation. MacArthur refused chloroform and gripped the chair as he endured the pain without wincing, while streams of blood and pus ran down his cheeks. When it was all over, MacArthur asked about the fee. The answer was, "Nothing, to a man like you."

Today, as we walk the quiet streets of Maitland, it is well to remember the courage of the men and women of former times who brought their "town" honor, importance and wealth in the great days of sail.

NOTES

1. McKiel, Rex, East Hants Historical Society, March 13, 1973.
2. The report of the *Milton* was first researched and reported by Archibald McMechan, and has been included in his articles and books over a period of years. This chapter is a summary of McMechan's report of the adventure. All quotes are from his text.
3. *Ibid.*

Joseph Howe
Notman's Photography, about 1871

CHAPTER TWELVE

JOE HOWE COMES TO MAITLAND

THE GREAT tribune of Nova Scotia, Joseph Howe was probably in the town of Maitland on many occasions during his life both as a journalist and politician. His career spanned the great years of a community that had grown in industry and wealth to be one of Nova Scotia's most prosperous towns.

Howe would have known men like W.D. Lawrence, the Roys and MacDougalls as well. He was a reformer and in essence the founder of the Liberal party. Howe had been a great promoter of industry and Maitland was a business oriented town.

Howe was a great politician. He knew all the tricks and devices that make men popular at the polls. Dale Carnegie might have learned something from the wily old campaigner. Yet, he had the best interests of his province at heart and he had more native ability in speaking and politics than any of his contemporaries.

Howe was idolized in many areas of the province and Maitland was known as a Liberal town. The crowds which came to hear the great orator were so large that on one occasion a platform was built on the second story of Isaac Douglas' blacksmith shop so that Howe could be seen by the huge assembly.

Howe was idolized, as a sports figure or rock star would be today. He had a very charming and attractive personality. So much so that on more than one occasion women named their children after him, giving them the surname Howe.

The men of Maitland were not uninformed. They were businessmen who had travelled the world, seen how affairs were run in Britain, France, the Orient and the United States. They were knowledgeable, wise and hard men who had faced and bested the sharpest con men in the trading ports of the world. They would not long be taken in by Howe's political craft, his good humour, jokes and backslapping. Yet they recognized his superior qualities.

SUPPER WITH JOE HOWE

Some years ago I was sent a letter from a Hants County councillor, Roma White, which exemplifies Howe's popularity in that constituency. It is now on public record in the Nova Scotia archives. It is the story of a visit by Joseph Howe to a home in what is now East Hants and demonstrates Howe's great courtesy and political skill. The story is related by Mrs. Alice Reid of Moose Brook, as told to her by her grandmother:

> At one time Joseph Howe represented Hants Co., in the local House of Assembly and during the election campaign, he was driving from Halifax to Windsor and as it was about supper time, he drove up to my grandmother's home, knocked and asked if he could have his horse put in the stable and fed and could he also have some supper.
>
> My grandmother already had a table set which was a large pot of corn meal porridge cooked upon the stove and was about to fill the numerous bowls for the family's supper.

She told Mr. Howe she could give him a share of what she had and while the horse was being attended to she hastily removed the everyday dishes, spread the best linen table cloth, dusted off her willow pattern dishes, rushed to the cellar and brought up a bottle of strawberry preserves, which she noticed was the last one she had. The precious pat of butter, reserved only for company, was placed on the table and the best the home provided was spread for the honored guest. Meanwhile the pot of porridge had been put out of sight.

When the table was ready, she just had time to smooth down her hair and put on her best white apron, when Mr. Howe arrived from the barn, washed, took his seat at the table, asked the blessing, then looked around and said, "When I first came in here I saw a pot of corn meal porridge cooking on the stove. Couldn't I have some of it?" My grandmother replied, "Oh, yes, if you would like it, but I don't usually serve it to company."

She filled the bowls with the porridge, which was still hot and they all ate it, probably enjoying it more than any they had ever eaten.

I don't know how many votes would have been forthcoming from that home, but I imagine Mr. Howe got them. At any rate Howe won the election with a majority of 383 over his opponent, Monson Goudge … (in 1856)

Alice B. Reid
Moose Brook, Hants Co.

In 1869, the old master met an entirely different situation in Maitland. This was now a very wealthy town and its wealth had been built upon world trade, not upon trading with the other provinces of the new nation called Canada.

When Howe arrived on an election tour, he met a host of well-informed men, who had prospered rapidly by trading in

Great Britain, the United States, France, China and the West Indies — in fact the four corners of the globe.

The now prosperous community, looking back on its early struggles, was naturally hostile to any movement that would threaten its future growth. It was said that the new nation, Canada, would limit Nova Scotia's growth and would reduce it to a poor cousin of Upper Canada. This in fact happened.

Howe himself had been leader of the anti-confederation movement and had travelled to England attempting to have the confederation reversed. He had been the champion of anti-confederation. Now, however, only a year later, he reversed his decision and, in fact, was running in a federal by-election under John A. Macdonald's Tories. Many branded him a turncoat. Others said he was bribed with offers of federal appointments. After thirty years in politics, mainly as champion of the common man of his province, Howe now returned again seeking election and was surrounded by enemies, who often had been his former supporters.

Joseph Shull in *Weekend Magazine*, in 1956, relates an event that took place at his grandfather's farm at Maitland during the 1869 by-election.[1]

There was to be a rally at Maitland in the dead of winter. Shull writes:

> Gramp's farm was on the edge of Maitland and he was hurrying up with the chores the morning the sleigh came by... He noticed the horse was limping. There had been sleighs and cutters going by all morning.
>
> The big meeting was on for that night... Goudge and Annand and Vail and Jones — all the big guns of the anti-Confederates — were in town already and they hadn't been wasting any time. Every tavern was jammed full and money was flowing free. Some loud-mouths were talking of tar and feathers for Joe when he got in.

Getting out of the cutter was Joe Howe. "Arthur," he said, "It's good to see you. That horse couldn't have thrown a shoe at a better place. Get me in out of this cold and give me a sip of something."

Howe was gray and pale and at sixty-five, looked exhausted by the long, cold campaign.

But to Howe's surprise, the old friend did not smile or extend a hand, and worse he refused to shoe the horse, and Howe was forced to walk into Maitland.

His reception at the hall was no better. His opponents had all the support and shouts of "liar," "turncoat,", "traitor" rang out.

In the middle of an opponent's speech, Howe got up quietly from his chair and wrapped himself closer in his buffalo coat and lay down on the bare boards of the platform, for he was exhausted.

There was a startled murmur in the hall and then a derisive chant began, "Get up, get up." Joe Howe had been driven to his last trick — he was playing on them for sympathy. Morrison, the speaker, took his cue from the angry audience and practically stood over Howe and went on with his harangue, pointing out that the bundled up, motionless figure in the baffalo coat was a renegade and a traitor.[2]

This is the version of the event Joseph Shull reports as handed down to him by his grandfather.

However, two versions of where this event took place exist. There is no doubt that Howe did come to Maitland and spoke there during the campaign. He had come around the Cobequid shore and spoke at Walton and Noel, then to Maitland, Kennetcook, and Nine Mile River.

James Roy, in his book *Joseph Howe,* paints a similar picture of Howe's last and most difficult campaign:

The picture of the campaign drawn by Johnson is a

> pathetic one... The weary and suffering old man driving hither and thither from township to township, exposing himself to the bitter winter weather, regardless of consequences, and carried through by the force of his indomitable will...
>
> Howe went to the hall, suffering acutely; sat in his chair for a time, listening to his rivals' torrents of vituperation, until, overcome with pain, he wrapped himself in his sleigh robe and lay down at the back of the platform while his opponents seemed literally to be dancing on his prostrate form.
>
> When it came his turn to reply, he pulled himself together with a supreme effort of will, read the sympathy in the faces of his farmer audience, and immediately the orator reasserted himself. Overcoming his bodily weakness he stood on the front of the platform, and, grasping the lapels of his coat in his familiar manner, he proceeded to pour forth his wrath and his humour on his commonplace opponents, who literally melted away into oblivion under his scathing attack.[3]

Howe won the election by 383 voters. But no doubt that cold winter's night in Hants was one of the most difficult in his long career. To the businessmen of Hants, who knew their industry and community were threatened, confederation was a hard sell, even for the tribune of Nova Scotia, Joseph Howe.

On May 6, 1873, Howe was appointed Lieutenant Governor of Nova Scotia. He died within days, on June 1, 1873, late at night at his residence — Government House on Barrington Street, Halifax.

Ironically, Joe Howe's connection with Maitland does not end there. His grandson, Captain Joseph Howe, was a resident of Maitland, as was Captain Howe's father, Edward Howe. Captain Howe was the master of the great Roy vessel, *Norwood*, when it was wrecked.

Even in my time there was still a resident in Maitland who bore the Howe name. Mr. J. Gordon Howe was a businessman living there in the 1960s. Howe House still exists and is preserved in Maitland.[4]

NOTES

1. Joseph Shull, "The Night They Killed Joe Howe," *Weekend Magazine*, Vol. 6, No. 26, 1956.
2. *Ibid.*
3. James Roy, *Joseph Howe.* Toronto: MacMillan, 1935, p. 285.
4. Hattie Densmore, Halifax *Chronicle-Herald*, 8 Feb. 1964.

CHAPTER THIRTEEN

ECONOMIC DECLINE: THE LONG SUNSET

MAITLAND did not collapse and disappear as did the Hants County ghost town of Renfrew. Rather, economic activity subsided over a long period of almost fifty years. The shipyards, the gypsum works, the wharves, the bank, the ferry, the Ship's Registry, eventually ceased to operate. The tennis courts, played on by the heirs of wealth, were finally abandoned.

The hundreds of transient shipyard workers left with the building of the last ships. The Commercial Hotel ceased to receive salesmen, politicians and visiting businessmen attending upon the wealthy Maitland clientele.

Tracks of the Midland Railway, whose trains once whistled and hissed as they steamed into the South Maitland station, have disappeared. The steel rails have been torn up and taken for salvage leaving a broad roadbed crossing through the wilderness.

It was not the fault of the men who still lived there that the economy of Maitland collapsed. In age, they were still sound businessmen and investors, though not as daring as in youth. They and their heirs wisely invested their money in bank and other stock and in bonds and sound investments. They lived their declining years in wealth and could pass that wealth on to their heirs.

An excellent picture of Maitland at the turn of the century exists in the *Halifax Herald* of Tuesday, August 8, 1899. Beneath a line-drawing of Alfred Putnam, "one of the shareholders of the Midland Railway Company," and also Vice president, is a vivid description of Maitland and district:

> If I were asked to name one of the very prettiest villages in Nova Scotia, I should unhesitatingly and quickly say — Maitland.
>
> Its approaches are beautiful. Comfortable and luxurious-looking houses; rich fields on both sides of the road up from Noel — well cultivated uplands on one side, and fertile marsh and dyke on the other.
>
> Selma is happy and contented looking, and its beauty prepares one for the more imposing liveliness of Maitland.
>
> Maitland's homes are full of plenty. Poverty is a very rare commodity, if it exists at all. Want of ample supply of the necessaries of life is unknown. There are not so many people in Maitland as there once were. Some empty houses may be seen. But the homes of Maitland are the abodes of comfort, and luxury is common. Many fine farms are here and it is well that this is so, for agriculture must now henceforth be a Mainland mainstay.

For a brief period, the construction of the Midland Railway provided an economic stimulus to the area. Alfred Putnam, former MP, and other investors of Maitland tried to revive the economy by backing the new railway. Even though the railway passed through South Maitland and provided short-term employment and improved transportation, it was no replacement for the shipbuilding industry.

The *Halifax Herald* correspondent mentioned above asks prophetically, in 1899:

> What of the future? ...Before a Midland Railway branch is built to Maitland (itself), there may be an application of some new method. Methods of transportation are so improving that some other means of transit than by a steam railroad may be discovered and utilized... These are the days of electric trolley lines and compressed air.

It was not the electric trolley or compressed air, but the gasoline engine and Henry Ford that changed transportation — but still it did not help Maitland recover its lost industry.

Many of the industrial leaders of Maitland lived well into the twentieth century. Their judgement was still sound and they retained their wealth and managed it well.

WEALTH REMAINS

The *Halifax Herald* correspondent in 1899 wrote of Maitland: "She is rich. Her people have many fine farms and few mortgages... The people of Maitland have on deposit in the Savings bank of the village no less than $300,000." In today's money this would be between fifteen and thirty million, for men in those years earned about one dollar per day for ten hours.

Through shrewd and conservative finance, the money often stayed with families for generations. Thus the village with its magnificent homes could be preserved. Servants could be retained, and economic life, though gradually declining, could go on.

FROZEN IN TIME

Through these financial resources and the dedicated work of the town fathers, the village and its magnificent homes, its stores, churches, the Commercial Hotel, streets and magnificent graveyards have been preserved. Maitland is

The old bank building, built 1860s-70s, is on the left.
Next to it on the right is the Frieze and Roy Store, built circa 1839.
This is how they appear today.

David Frieze House, shown here in a recent photo,
was also the Commercial Hotel. It was built circa 1835.

Foley house, built circa 1870,
is currently a bed and breakfast, and restaurant.

William D. Lawrence house, built circa 1870,
the home of the great shipbuilder and politician.
The house is currently a provincial museum.

Howe house was built circa 1859.
This home was used by the descendants of Hon. Joseph Howe.

This impressive mansion, called Springhurst,
was the home of Alfred Putnam, and built circa 1870.

**Murphy house (Oakdale) was built circa 1850.
It is currently the home of Fred and Christie Roy.**

Captain William Douglas house, 1860s. The widow's walk, or small tower on the top of the house, is still preserved. From this, Mrs. Douglas and children would anxiously watch the bay for the captain's safe return.

Dr. Brown house, built in the 1860s.

Captain Jack Putnam house, built circa 1878.

The highly decorated Dickey house was the home of a master carpenter with a passion for external decoration. Thomas Dickey even delighted in elaborate gingerbread designs on barns and work buildings. This Gothic Revival house has a steeply pitched cross-gable roof with prominent pointed gables. This house is a classic example of Gothic Revival.

substantially as it was one hundred years ago. A walk through the tree-lined streets is a walk back into the past century. It is a village frozen in time.

Frieze and Roy's store is still intact. The Commercial Hotel building has been preserved. Foley House is intact and operating as a guest house and restaurant. The mansion of W.D. Lawrence now operates as a provincial museum. Each of the Victorian homes that line the streets are preserved and their historic owners known. The home of Captain Howe, an heir of Joseph Howe, still stands as does that of the master builder, Lockhart Lawrence. The Putnam mansion is a large, perfectly preserved example of classical revival style. Oakdale, presently occupied by Mr. and Mrs. Fred Roy, is a striking and unique example of Maitland's homes.

I have crossed the same thresholds and entered the same rooms as Joseph Howe did so long ago. To visit Maitland is to reach back and touch the historic past of Nova Scotia in the great days of sail.

Outside the village, along the Cobequid shore and in Noel, are the perfectly preserved homes of the "rich and famous" of the nineteenth century. The majestic home of Alfred Putnam, MP, is preserved with meticulous care.

Remarkably, Maitland and its historic buildings have remained intact eighty years after the last of the shipbuilders have passed from the scene. Cultural roots and traditions run deep in Maitland and pride in the great achievements of those who have gone before is paramount.

Old records and photographs are carefully preserved and historical societies have recorded information which might have passed from human memory.

Recently a scientific inventory of historic buildings has been taken and the village declared a Heritage Conservation District. Hopefully, we are thus assured that this unique historic treasure — the birthplace and home of the Iron Men in the days of sail and the haven of the Bluenose Master Mariner — may be preserved for future generations.

CHAPTER FOURTEEN

THE BAT CAVES

ANY RECORD of the Maitland area would be incomplete without some mention of the mysterious Hayes Cave — the home of bats and porcupines. It is also a concrete reminder of the days when gypsum was king, since the caves are a natural feature of the gypsum hills, and a wall of white gypsum rock can still be seen from the old site of Hayes farm near South Maitland.

On the banks of Five Mile River, mountains of white gypsum rock stand in contrast to the green hills. The bat caves, more commonly known as Hayes Cave, are near the abandoned Midland Railway line at the isolated site of Hayes farm, in an area known as Maple Grove.

The cave is part of the gypsum deposit that were so important to the early settlers of Maitland. The adjacent land, formerly a farm, was cultivated between 1827 and the 1940s. Cattle and vegetables were raised on the farm and at one time the cave entrance was so large that hay wagons used to enter it. Because of rockfalls, the entrance was considerably smaller when I visited the cave.

The largest known cave in Nova Scotia, it is more than 1,115 feet long — almost a quarter of a mile. It is 82 feet (25 meters) wide for large portions of its length. Height is variable, ranging from 42 feet (13 meters) in the first chamber

An identified boy at the mouth of Hayes Cave, circa 1901.
Courtesy of East Hants Historical Society

to less than three feet (1 meter) but, on average, ranges from 13 to 20 feet (6 meters).

This remarkable natural phenomenon has now been protected by the provincial government, since the Hayes farm area contains a number of unique species of plants and animals.

The outstanding feature of the cave is the absolute lack of light. If your flashlight fails, you are in total blackness and cannot see a step ahead or your hand before you. Thus the cave is frightening to many, and this fear is exacerbated by the common belief that flashlights have been known to suddenly die in the cave's dank atmosphere.

Also, there is a lack of sound, except for the regular

dripping, winter and summer, of seeping water which falls into the miniature lakes in the different chambers; or, if bats are disturbed, there is a muffled swoosh as shadows flicker in the eerie amber glow of the flashlight.

The temperature is remarkably constant. In winter it may be 6 or 7 degrees celsius and in August it is roughly the same. This even temperature is ideal for the bats. The spelunker first notices the dank atmosphere and the chill, since the relative humidity is always 100 percent.

The water in the miniature lakes in the various cave chambers is the same temperature as the air and varies in depth. It rises and falls as much as two meters depending on rainfall. Under the domes of the caves, the shores of the lakes are sloped and slippery with slime and mud. Obtaining a handhold is not always easy.

Of real concern to anyone exploring the cave is the presence of high radioactivity. A government report indicates that visitors, even authorized ones, could be harmed by the effects of radon gas. Radon gas, one of the by-products of uranium decay, has been detected in very high concentrations. The alpha-emitting radon gas has been detected in concentrations of 10-20 times that of the air outside the cave.[1]

BATS

The most remarkable feature of this ancient cave is the bats, which cling in clusters to the walls. In 1983, in zone C alone, there were 4,740 bats counted and, while zones A to E had fewer, estimates and counts of hibernating bats in Hayes Cave from 1963 to 1983 reached as high as eight thousand. These figures were often verified by double counts.[2]

The great concern for the provincial government today is to control the unique nature of the cave and the bat population.

THE DONCASTER EXPEDITION

Surely Hayes Cave must be one of the most gruesome, dangerous and eerie places in Nova Scotia. As I entered the mouth, it was as if I was entering the portals of Hell. The flashlight beam penetrates the blackness and scans the damp walls of gypsum and rock. Dripping water strikes your helmet and your breath, in the confined stale air, becomes short. It is the subterranean world of Jules Verne. One is also gripped, however, by a mad sense of reckless adventure.

Though spelunking in the cave is now forbidden, on April 17, 1987, I joined an expedition which was led by an intrepid spelunker, Roger Doncaster, a man of about twenty-three.

The small company rendezvoued at Hill's store in South Maitland, just across from the site of the former Midland Railway station and on the Hants side of the Goss Bridge. Seven persons entered the cave, three of them women, one of whom was a young doctor of about twenty-seven.

The opening in the mountainside is now reduced to a five- by two-foot slit. My notes made at the time indicate that "the gypsum beneath your feet slopes and so, by holding the sides, you gradually lower yourself eight feet to a landing in the darkness." This first landing is the vestibule of the main chamber.

The first vault appeared to be about thirty feet high and about sixty feet wide and is elongated as the cave goes deeper into the gypsum mountain.

In the vestibule we organized our gear and accustomed ourselves to the darkness. We unpacked flashlights, ropes, gloves and first aid equipment. Hardhats were a necessary precaution for rockfalls and dripping water. We needed good gripping boots, plus warm and waterproof jackets.

We stood beside the lake or pond, which at the edge is quite shallow, but might reach four or five feet in depth and is very clear. It is about twenty-five feet at its greatest width but runs about two-thirds of the cave's length.

Leaving the main chamber and following the shore, you are then in darkness; but, with lights out, you can see a glimmer of light in the water reflecting the distant opening. When you make the first turn you leave the reflection behind and are engulfed by moist blackness and the sound of water dripping on gypsum stones.

After the first chamber, the cave narrows and the floor becomes a jumble of slanting, greasy boulders, frequently covered with half an inch of mud.

We walked in line, flashlight beams moving even deeper into the crevices. The light is a lifeline. One went out — another was dropped. Often the flashlight can drop twenty feet. While I was working up a tunnel my light slipped from my pocket, leaving me for a moment in the inky darkness. Luckily, Guy, a Quebecer behind me, caught it before it hit rock.

Local residents had warned me some time before that lights mysteriously go out in the cave, but mine worked well. They mentioned also that years ago a Mi'kmaq had gone into the cave and was never seen again. Groping in the darkness, I could well imagine how this could happen if you were alone and without light.

One of the three women noticed that something brushed by her cheek. Soon we discovered that bats, attracted by the lights, were swooping around us. Flashing the lights along the white ceiling, now less than eight feet high, we saw hanging in profusion, like grapes, hundreds of bats — not large, but almost mouse-size — dangling by their feet, some apparently still in hibernation.

At midway, the footing became even more precarious. As we moved from boulder to boulder, the ceiling was frequently close to our heads and the cave narrowed. The clank of helmets hitting hanging rocks surprised us.

In the next chamber I noted that breathing became difficult. There seemed no exit, but we finally found a rock-strewn sloping tunnel ascending upward almost thirty feet, but so narrow that your pack scraped the roof as you climbed. It was so small you could brace yourself and climb easily. Those behind shone the light so you could see for finding foot and hand holds. Once up, the first climber provided light for the others. You could not carry a light since both hands were needed in climbing.

Finally Doncaster informed us we had reached the end of the cave. I could see no possible exit. Low tunnels of less than three feet fingered off in two directions. They lead to dead ends.

The ladies, considering the difficulties, seemed in especially good cheer and, using flash cameras, began to take photos. As the lights popped and others clambered about, I hoped that the activities would not loosen the mud and gypsum and send portions of the roof caving in on us. I wondered then if our guide had been wise enough to inform anyone of our whereabouts, and the joviality in such a serious situation made me begin to question his judgement.

However, in a few minutes, he directed us to a narrowing two-foot escape tunnel, which was a relief for I had no enthusiasm for a return journey.

The exit was another vertical climb, known as the "chimney," with little room for movement. Claustrophobia becomes a problem as you cannot lift your arms in the cramped tunnel.

Up we went, crawling through muck-covered rock, slanting this way and that, gripping with toes and fingers for a hold, easing the body along the rock for greater friction to prevent a slip back down twenty feet.

The tunnel was too small for the packs and too steep at the final chimney that led us out, so we passed the bags up by human chain to those out first.

The final collar that led to open air on the side of the mountain was in places little wider than my shoulders. I could not use my arms at first since I could not put them before me, and therefore couldn't climb.

By taking off the helmet, placing one arm ahead and gaining foot purchase on a rock, I neared daylight. Now my head was out. Now an arm. I squirmed and pushed with my feet and finally popped out to find a thirty-foot bank and a drop below to be avoided. It was a great relief to reach fresh air and daylight again.

The first out gathered our cameras and equipment and photographed those squirming like ants from the bowels of the earth. All made it intact. No one was injured or lost.

What did I make of the trip? Let's say, it was a trip I will never forget. However, I suspect it may be some time, some considerable time, before I have the desire to venture into Hayes Cave again.

The bat caves, while not of great historical significance, are none-the-less another fascinating feature of the Maitland district.

NOTES

1. Hayes Cave Study, 1963, N.S. Dept. of Mines.
2. *Ibid.*

APPENDIX A

DOUGLAS TOWNSHIP ASSESSMENT FOR 1795

	Pounds	Shilling	Pence
Noel District	4	9	4
Kennetcook District	3	17	2 1/2
Nine Mile River District	3	6	2
Shubenacadie District	2	10	2 1/2
	14	2	11

Anthony, John (Senior) .... Kennetcook
Anthony, Noah .... Kennetcook
Archibald, John .... Noel
Barbrick, Jenj. or Benonoi .... Kennetcook
Barkley, Alex .... Nine Mile River
Blois, Abraham .... Kennetcook
Cameron, Alex .... Noel
Campbell, James .... Kennetcook
Carr, Archibald .... Noel
Chisholm, William .... Nine Mile River
Colter, John .... Kennetcook
Dalrymple, James .... Kennetcook
Densmore, Francis .... Noel
Densmore, James Sen. .... Noel
Densmore, James (Junior) .... Noel
Densmore, Samuel Jun. .... Noel

Densmore, Wm. Sen .... Noel
Drisket, James .... Noel
Duglass, James .... Noel blacksmith
Eakins, Grake .... Nine Mile River
Ellis, James .... Shubenacadie
England, Abraham .... Kennetcook (shown with Abr. Blois)
Ettinger, Lewis .... Kennetcook
Faulkner, Robert .... Noel
Faulkner, Thomas .... Noel
Faulkner, Wm. .... Noel
Ferguson, Alex .... Nine Mile River
Ferguson, John .... Nine Mile River
Ferguson, John .... Nine Mile River
Fraser, James .... Nine Mile River
Fraser, Neil .... Nine Mile River
Grant, Alex .... Nine Mile River
Grant, Donald .... Nine Mile River
Gill, William .... Kennetcook
Graham, John .... Kennetcook
Hay, Patrick .... Shubenacadie
Hennigar, Christian .... Kennetcook
Higgins, James .... Kennetcook
Hurley, Patrick .... Shubenacadie
Hynds, John .... Kennetcook
Jackson, Stephen .... Noel
Kenty, Terrence .... Shubenacadie
Laffin, Thomas .... Kennetcook
Lehey, John .... Kennetcook
McArthur, Allen .... Shubenacadie
McArthur, Duncan .... Nine Mile River
McCalum, Alex .... Noel
Macculloch, Alex .... Kennetcook
McDonald, Alex. Sen .... Kennetcook
McDonald, Alex. ? .... Kennetcook
McDonald, Andrew .... Shubenacadie

McDonald, Angus..........Nine Mile River
McDonald, Donald..........Nine Mile River
McDonald, Donald..........Kennetcook
McDonald, Duncan..........Nine Mile River
McDonald, James..........Shubenacadie
Macdonald, John Sen...........Kennetcook
Macdonald, John Jun...........Kennetcook
MacDonald, John..........Nine Mile River
Macdonald, Patrick..........Kennetcook
McDonald, William..........Shubenacadie
McDougals, Donald..........Nine Mile River
McDougale, Daniel..........Nine Mile River
McDougald, Evan..........Nine Mile River
McDougall, William..........Shubenacadie
McFee, Evan..........Nine Mile River
McFee, James..........Nine Mile River
McFee, John..........Nine Mile River
McFee, John..........Nine Mile River
McKenzie, Adam..........Noel
McKenzie, Donald..........Nine Mile River
McKenzie, Donald..........Noel
McKenzie, Duncan..........Nine Mile River
McKenzie, Kenneth..........Nine Mile River
McKenzie, Kenneth..........Noel
McKenzie, Malcolm..........Nine Mile River
McLaughlin, Laughlin..........Nine Mile River
McNaughton, Alex..........Nine Mile River
McNeil, John..........Nine Mile River
MacLean, Hector Esq...........Kennetcook
MacLearn, Mathew..........Kennetcook
McQueen, Donald..........Shubenacadie
Main, Andrew, Sen...........Noel
Main, Andrew, Jun...........Noel
Main, George..........Shubenacadie
Mason, Conrad..........Kennetcook

Miller, George .... Kennetcook
Moore, John .... Shubenacadie
Moore, Joseph .... Shubenacadie
Morris, John .... Noel
Nellson, William .... Shubenacadie
Neil, John .... Noel cooper
O'Brien, Andrew .... Noel
O'Brien, Isaac .... Noel
O'Brien, Jacob .... Noel
O'Brien, Robert .... Noel
Pressley, James .... Noel
Putnam, Caleb .... Noel
Quirk, Peirce .... Noel shoemaker
Rafter, John .... Nine Mile River
Rose, Donald .... Shubenacadie
Ryan, John .... Kennetcook
Rupel, Joseph .... Nine Mile River
Ryan, Joseph .... Kennetcook
Ryans, John Sen. .... Kennetcook
Ryans, John Jun. .... Kennetcook
Ryans, Thomas .... Kennetcook
Scott, Archibald .... Nine Mile River
Sheild, John .... Kennetcook
Singer, Mrs. .... Kennetcook
Smith, Caleb .... Noel
Smith, John .... Noel
Smith, John .... Kennetcook
Smith, William Esq. .... Kennetcook
Thomson, Donald .... Nine Mile River
Wardrobe, James .... Shubenacadie
Welsh, Thomas .... Nine Mile River
Whedon, Capt. David .... Noel
White, George .... Kennetcook
Williams, James .... Shubenacadie
Williams, John .... Shubenacadie

Williams, John..Noel
Woodworth, Paul..Shubenacadie
Woodworth, Stephen ....Shubenacadie

— courtesy John V. Duncanson

APPENDIX B

PARTIAL LIST OF SHIPS BUILT IN MAITLAND DISTRICT

Name	Builder
Hemisphere (1843)	David Crowe
Fowler (1849)	Charles Cox
Rainbow (1846)	Arch McCallum
Douglas (1846)	Adam Douglas
Noel (1849)	
Argo (1851)	Wm. McDougall
Nautilius (1851)	David Frieze
Time (1855)	
St. Lawrence (1852)	W.D. Lawrence
Architect (1855)	W.D. Lawrence
Defiance (1856)	Robert Esdale
Charles Adams (1857)	Arch. McCallum
Aleppo (1858)	Alexander Roy
Hedley Vicars (1859)	
Persia (1859)	W.D. Lawrence

Vessels Built in the 1860s

Wave (1860)	A.G. O'Brien
Clyde (1860)	Alexander Ross
Jane (1861)	G.B. McLellan
Autumn (1861)	John Neil
Agile (1861)	George Dart
Alice (1861)	Sydney Smith

Syrpus (1861)	Alexander Roy
Advent (1861)	John R. Crowe
Craigrownie (1863)	A.A. McDougall
Aurora (1862)	John McDougall
Breeze (1862)	Wm. McDougall
J.B. Eliot (1862)	Alexander Ross
Lily (1862)	George O. Smith
W.G. Putnam (1862)	W.D. Lawrence
Adelaide (1862)	James Douglas
Ann (1863)	Arch McCallum
Ariomede (1863)	David Crowe
Cyrene (1863)	Alexander Roy
Emily (1863)	
Jessie (1863)	A.A. McDougall
Mary (1863)	W.D. Lawrence
Mozart (1863)	Sydney Smith
Stranger	Joseph Monteith
Amanda Jane (1863)	Osmond O'Brien
Asia (1863)	Faulkner & Smith (Bowden)
Eureka (1863)	Levi Densmore
Tweed (1863)	Wm. McDougall
Agnes (1864)	Arch McCallum
Blonde (1864)	Alexander Roy
D.B.R. (1864)	A.A. McDougall
Magna Charta (1864)	Sydney Smith
Horton (1864)	Fred Brown
Zephyr (1864)	Alexander Roy
Lara (1864)	Jos. Monteith
Naiad (1864)	J.E. O'Brien
Petrel (1864)	S.D. Brown
Dayspring (1864)	J.E. O'Brien
Hunter (1864)	Wm. Hunter & Others
Minnehaha (1864)	Joseph Wier registered owner
Medora (1865)	John Neil
Mary (1865)	A.A. McDougall

Aspen (1865)	Joseph Miller
Brenda (1865)	Charles Cox
Duncan (1865)	James McDougall
Wild Horse (1865)	John Macomber
John Geddie (1866)	Wm. McDougall
Nancy (1866)	John Trahey
Alice Roy (1866)	Alexander Roy
Nazarene (1866)	Matthew Murphy & Others
June Ure (1866)	A.A. McDougall
Scotia Queen (1867)	George O. Smith
Northern Light (1866)	Wm. Hamilton & R. Smith
Bluenose (1867)	John Sanderson
Annie (1867)	Alfred Putnam
Maggie (1867)	David Dart
Pegasus (1867)	W.D. Lawrence
Lavinia (1868)	David Dart
Bina (1868)	A.A. McDougall
Seaforth (1868)	Charles Cox
Era (1869)	John Trahey
Armanilla (1869)	David Dart
Maggie Brown (1869)	A.A. McDougall
Ella (1868)	Joseph Monteith
A.D. Whidden (1869)	Wm. Moore
Hudson (1868)	Charles Cox
Stella Lodge (1869)	Donald McDougall
Fresh Breeze (1869) launched same day as *Stella Lodge*	Wm. McDougall
M.E. Cox (1869)	Charles Cox
Mary A. Nelson (1868)	John Trahey
Mary (1865)	W.D. Lawrence
Wanderer (1864)	George O. Smith

Vessels without date: the *Chief, Clifton, Robert Boak, Zero, Mary, Colchester* all built by Matthew Norris. *Blanche* built by Arch. Cox. *Julia* and *Spartan* by Charles Cox. *Brimage* built by

S.D. Brown. The *Orkney* owned by the Crowes of Selma. *Industry*, Captain Ezra McDougall; *Buffalo*, Captain Sam Nelson.

Vessels Built in the 1870s

(Barques and Full-Rigged Ships)

Algonquin (1870)	Charles Cox
Minnie Graham (1870)	A.A. McDougall
Huron (1870)	Alexander Roy
Edward (1870)	Alfred Putnam
Peerless (1870)	Sydney Smith
Nancy Ross (1870)	Alexander Ross
Elizabeth Ann (1870)	James Moore
Forest Chief (1870)	John Sanderson
Reasylvius (1870)	Brown & Anthony
Pactolus (1870)	Osmond O'Brien
Midas (1870)	Arch. McCallum
Maitland (1871)	George O. Smith & Son
Ruby (1871)	Wm. McDougall
Eliza Campbell (1871)	A.A. McDougall
Mary Jane (1871)	L. Lawrence
Edward Barrow (1871)	John Trahey
Amelia Ann (1871)	John Clark
Medusa (1871)	Arch McCallum
Maggie Elliot (1872)	Alexander Ross
Harold (1872)	J. Sanderson
Lillian M. Vigus (1872)	John Trahey
Algoma (1872)	Arch. McCallum
Jane Campbell (1872)	A.A. McDougall
Puskatqua (1872)	Osmond O'Brien
Cupid (1872)	Bowden, Smith & Pratt
Snow Queen (1872)	Alexander Roy
Tranmere (1872)	Geo. O. Smith & Son
Lara (1872)	J. Monteith
George (1872)	Alfred Putnam

Lotus (1872)	Pratt & Cox
Edith (1872)	James Douglas
Lady Vere de Vere (1873)	Geo. O. Smith & Son
Truro (1873)	John Sanderson
MacDougall (1873)	Wm. McDougall
Umavar (1873)	L. O'Brien
Lottie (1873)	W.P. Cameron
Eva (1873)	James McDougall
Disco (1873)	A.A. McDougall
Princeport (1874)	Matthew Morris
W.H. Corsar (1874)	S.D. Brown
Sarah Allen (1874)	Osmond O'Brien
Maggie E. Seed (1874)	Alfred Putnam
Isabella Ure (1874)	A.A. McDougall
W.D. Lawrence (2459 tons) (1874)	W.D. Lawrence
Hannah D (1874)	Robert Densmore
Francis Herbert (1874)	Cox & Pratt
Silas Curtis (1874)	Geo. O. Smith & Son
Charles Cox (1875)	Charles Cox
Colchester (1875)	John Sanderson
Cromarty (1875)	James Rose
Emeline (1875)	Joseph Monteith
Dunselaw (1875)	H.D. Arthur
Laura Emily (1875)	W. Bowden Smith
Wm. Douglas (1875)	Alexander Roy
Margaret Mitchell (1875)	A.A. McDougall
Noel (1875)	Osmond O'Brien
Maggie O'Brien (1875)	Lorenzo O'Brien
Annie Putnam (1875)	Alfred Putnam
Hecla (1875)	Adams McDougall
John Lorway (1875)	John Trehey
Capri (1875)	Joseph Monteith
Numa (1876)	George Douglas
Annie (1876)	Lockhart Lawrence

Minnie Swift (1876)	Charles Cox
Bessie (1876)	A.T. Dalrymple
John Trahey (1876)	John Trahey
Trust (1876)	Frieze and Roy
Joseph (1876)	Arch McCallum
Laura (1876)	R.F. Densmore
Norman (1876)	A.A. McDougall
Osmond O'Brien (1877)	O. O'Brien
Florence Abbott (1877)	Jas. Moore
Thomas E. Kenny (1877)	Alfred Putnam
Esther Roy (1877)	Alexander Roy
Erinna (1877)	S.D. Brown
Senator (1878)	Jos. Monteith
Margaret Craig (1878)	A.A. McDougall
Sherwood (1878)	Alfred Putnam
Scotland (1879)	James McDougall
Ada Brown (1879)	A.A. McDougall
Gloaming (1879)	Joseph Monteith
Zulu (1879)	Alfred Putnam
W.J. Stairs (1879)	Alexander Roy
Sylvan (1879)	Adams McDougall
Milton (1879)	Brown and Anthony

Vessels Built in the 1880s and '90s

Delhana (1880)	A.A. McDougall
Isabel (1880)	W.P. Cameron
Adele (1880)	Joseph Monteith
Minnie Brown (1881)	A.A. McDougall
Mauna Loa (1881)	Charles Putnam
M. & S. Cox (1881)	Charles Cox
Paragon (1881)	S.D. Brown
Alfred (1881)	O. O'Brien
Evivia (1880)	Wm. Ross
Maggie Dart (1882)	Robert Dart
Christina (1882)	A.A. McDougall

Strathome (1883)	Alfred Putnam
Amada (1883)	Osmond O'Brien
R. Morrow (1884)	Alexander Roy
Osberga (1884)	Adams McDougall
Linnet (1884)	W.P. Cameron
Grandee (1884)	Joseph Monteith
Advance (1884)	E. Densmore
Cragie Burn (1885)	A.A. McDougall
Lizzie (1885)	Charles Putnam
Man Zu (1855)	Charles Putnam
New Pactolus (1885)	Osmond O'Brien
Strathay (1880)	Alfred Putnam
Selkirk (1886)	W.P. Cameron
Linwood (1887)	Alexander Roy
Ensenda (1889)	W.P. Cameron
Calburga (1890)	Adams McDougall
E.A. O'Brien (1891)	Osmond O'Brien
Savona (1891)	W.P. Cameron
Earnscliffe (1891)	Joseph Monteith
Norwood (1891)	Alexander Roy
Launberga (1893)	Adams McDougall
Strathern (1893)	Alfred Putnam
Strathisia (1890)	Alfred Putnam

The year 1893 saw the last of the great freighting fleet of "deep-water" ships launched at Maitland. Since that date, with the exception of the barquentine *Ressie*, the only "white sails spread to the breeze" have been those of the goodly fleet of schooners engaged in trading and lumber carrying.

— courtesy Fred Roy